Design

At the end of World War I there was a widespread belief, particularly in Great Britain, that the pre-war naval arms race had been a significant factor in provoking the war. Among the victorious powers there were plans to rebuild or expand their navies, so the prospect of another costly competition in warship construction was both alarming and unwelcome, especially to the economically exhausted British. However, the Royal Navy wished to maintain its position of dominance and so encouraged discussions to limit the growth of navies. Battleships were the main consideration because of their enormous size and cost but cruisers also formed a significant part of these discussions.

In 1919 the British Government proposed that future naval estimates should be based on the assumption that no major war would occur within ten years – the 'ten year rule', which was not abandoned until 1932. The British planned an international conference to discuss 'Pacific and Far Eastern' affairs, an area of the world that the United States considered as their sphere of influence. The United States therefore proposed a naval limitation conference, to be held in Washington in 1921, invitations being sent to just Great Britain, France, Italy and Japan, although other countries were invited to attend relevant parts of the negotiations. It was not possible to agree a limit on the total tonnage of cruisers for each country but a limit on the size of individual vessels was agreed – a maximum displacement of 10,000 tons with guns no larger than 8 inches in calibre.

A conference held in Geneva in 1927 again attempted to agree a total tonnage but failed. The London Treaty of 1930 defined two different types of cruiser: 'heavy' cruisers with guns larger than 6.1 inches and 'light' cruisers with guns smaller than 6.1 inches. The total tonnage for each type was also agreed; in the case of Great Britain this was 146,800 tons for 'heavy' cruisers and 192,200 tons for 'light' cruisers. To comply with this agreement, the number of 'County' class cruisers ('A' cruisers) to be built was reduced, as was that of their smaller half-sisters, *York* and *Exeter* ('B' cruisers).

When the Admiralty first started their discussions after World War I regarding the future need for cruisers, it was assumed that the cost of cruisers required for trade protection in distant places would be provided by the relevant colonies, hence the cruisers were initially referred to as 'Colonial Cruisers'. The thirteen heavy cruisers comprising the resulting 'County' class fell into three sub-groups – the *Kent* class (*Berwick, Cornwall, Cumberland, Kent, Suffolk, Australia* and *Canberra*); the *London* class (*Devonshire, London, Shropshire* and *Sussex*); and the *Norfolk* class (*Dorsetshire* and *Norfolk*). As suggested by their names, *Australia* and *Canberra* were funded by Australia, the only part of the Empire to fulfil the expectations of the Admiralty.

These ships were designed under the Director of Naval Construction (DNC) Sir Eustace H Tennyson d'Eyncourt, initial design being by Charles Lillicrap, later to become DNC himself, with the detail design team led by William Berry, successor to d'Eyncourt as DNC. Being designed to the maximum dimensions allowed by the treaty, many felt the 'County' class were too

Cornwall in 1933 displaying the colours normally worn on the China Station – white hull and buff funnels. The awning over the quarterdeck, the boats hanging over the side, ready for lowering, the ship's boom and the accommodation ladder are all clearly visible. By this date the ship has a HACS on the after superstructure and a Type SIIL catapult.

Kent in 1928 as completed, with no aircraft or catapult. The HACS aft has yet to be fitted. *(National Maritime Museum N1757)*

large and expensive and that Great Britain would be better served by more, smaller cruisers, but the high freeboard with good seaworthiness proved very valuable. The main parameters as defined for the class were that the design was to include eight 8in guns and have a speed of 33 knots.

Preliminary calculations, for what was to become the *Kent* class, showed that little weight would be available for protection and hence the speed requirement was lowered

Officers stand watch on the bridge of *Suffolk* in 1933. *(via Hugh Williams)*

to 31 knots. This reduced the power required by 25 per cent and the weight of machinery by approximately 400 tons. It was eventually decided that within the same weight allowance slightly more power could be provided, giving an extra ½ knot of speed. The resulting vessels were 630ft overall (590ft between perpendiculars) with a beam of 68ft 3in.

The 'County' class featured a new design of forward superstructure incorporating the navigating bridge, wheelhouse, signalling and compass platforms and gunnery director in a single block. This rationalised the separate armoured conning tower and myriad of decks and mast platforms of previous designs. Deleting the fire control equipment from the mast enabled the heavy tripod masts to be replaced by lighter pole masts which were sufficient for signalling yards and the spread of wireless antennae.

In addition to the 8in guns, the armament included four 4in HA guns, two multiple pom-poms and two quadruple torpedo tubes. The protection for the main magazines was 4in on the sides with 3in elsewhere; the secondary magazines receiving one inch less. Machinery spaces were protected by a 1⅜in deck and 1in sides and bulkheads. The weight of armour was slightly in excess of 10 per cent of the displacement.

The *Kent* class were all completed in 1928, including the two ships funded by Australia, even though they had not been laid down until a year later than the others. The Australian ships had minor differences, including an additional light pole on the mainmast and taller funnels. The first group had external torpedo bulges but these were omitted in later ships, improving the lines and hence the speed.

The *London* class had a slightly increased length between perpendiculars, 595ft, with a reduced beam of 66ft, resulting in an increase in speed of ¾ knot. Other small changes were made to the design including moving the two forward

■ BUILDING DATA

Name	Builder	Laid Down	Launched
Kent class			
Berwick	Fairfield, Govan	15 September 1924	30 March 1926
Cornwall	Devonport Dockyard	9 October 1924	11 March 1926
Cumberland	Vickers Armstrong, Barrow	18 October 1924	16 March 1926
Kent	Chatham Dockyard	15 November 1924	16 March 1926
Suffolk	Portsmouth Dockyard	30 September 1924	16 February 1926
Australia	John Brown, Clydebank	26 August 1925	17 March 1927
Canberra	John Brown, Clydebank	9 September 1925	31 May 1927
London class			
Devonshire	Devonport Dockyard	16 March 1926	22 October 1927
London	Portsmouth Dockyard	23 February 1926	14 September 1927
Shropshire	Beardmore, Dalmuir	24 February 1927	5 July 1928
Sussex	Hawthorn Leslie	1 February 1927	22 February 1928
London class			
Dorsetshire	Portsmouth Dockyard	21 September 1927	29 January 1929
Norfolk	Fairfield, Govan	8 July 1927	12 December 1928

funnels and the two aft turrets aft. This group was completed in 1929.

The final two ships adopted a new design of turret for the primary armament. This turret was being designed for the smaller six-gun 'B' cruisers and was intended to reduce weight but actually increased it when finally built. The predicted weight saving was used to increase protection, resulting in the ships actually being slightly overweight when completed. Virtually identical to the *London* class, the rake of stem was slightly increased resulting in an increase in overall length. These ships were completed in 1930.

Propulsion was by means of four shafts, generally driven by two sets of Parsons turbines, through single reduction gears. *Berwick*, *Australia* and *Canberra* were fitted with Brown-Curtis, rather than Parsons, turbines. The turbines powering the wing shafts were located in the forward engine room and the eight boilers required were divided equally between two boiler rooms. The initial design included relatively short funnels but trials soon proved these to be impractical and hence their height was increased by 15ft, the two Australian ships having the height of their funnels increased by 18ft.

Weight saving measures included the use of 'high tensile' steel in the hull struc-

Canberra in July 1928 shows the additional pole topmast on the main. Like the other *Kent*s, the RAN 'Counties' also had their funnels raised, but to a slightly greater height than their RN sisters. *(Wright & Logan Collection)*

■ DESIGN CHARACTERISTICS

	Kent class	*London* class	*Norfolk* class
Displacement	9750-9870t (standard) 13,400-13,540t (deep)	9830-9850t (standard) 13,315t (deep)	9925-9975t (standard) 13,425t (deep)
Length (oa)	630-633ft	630-633ft	633-635.4ft
Length (pp)	590ft	595ft	595ft
Beam	68.3ft	66ft	66ft
Power	80,000shp	80,000shp	80,000shp
Speed	31.5 knots	32.25 knots	32.25 knots
Armament (as built)	4 x twin 8in/50 calibre Mk VIII guns (Mk I mountings for *Kent* and *London* classes, Mk II mountings for *Norfolk* class) 4 x 4in/45 calibre QF Mk V AA guns 4 x 2pdr pom-poms 2 x quadruple 21in torpedo tubes		

No aircraft facilities were included in the initial design but when trials revealed that the weight-saving measures had been successful, the support for a catapult, but not the catapult itself, was included.

Devonshire, of the second (or *London*) group, in 1929/30, showing her 'as-built' configuration with rangefinders either side of the bridge. The searchlights either side of the third funnel (moved from the after superstructure) was a recognition feature of this group. *(Wright & Logan Collection)*

ture and aluminium for non-structural members and fittings. Additionally, fir was used for the wooden decks instead of the usual teak. Stability was high, resulting in 'stiff' ships which made good gun platforms.

The primary armament comprised eight 8in 50cal Mk VIII guns in either twin Mk I or Mk II mountings, the former for the first two groups and the latter for the final pair, *Dorsetshire* and *Norfolk*. Both mountings had a maximum elevation of 70° and an intended rate of fire of 12 rounds a minute, a figure never achieved in practice. They were very complicated and each exceeded the original estimated weights by about 50 tons, the Mk I weighing 205 to 210 tons and the Mk II approximately 220 tons. The Mk II had a combined cordite and shell handling room whereas in the Mk I the shell handling room was located above the cordite handling room. This did however result in a larger base, approximately 14ft in diameter.

The *Kent* and *London* classes were fitted with a director control tower forward and another aft and a 12ft rangefinder either side of the upper bridge. The forward control towers of *Dorsetshire* and *Norfolk* had power training and an integral rangefinder.

Anti-aircraft defence was provided by just four single 4in 45cal Mk V guns on HA mountings, either Mk III or IV. Control was provided from a single High Angle Control System (HACS) Mk I, the director being located aft, although this was only fitted during build to *Shropshire*, *Sussex*, *Dorsetshire* and *Norfolk*, the others receiving theirs during suitable refits. Multiple pom-poms were specified for the ships but unavailable during build and hence all ships were initially fitted with four single 2pdr pom-poms.

Torpedo armament comprised two sets of quadruple torpedo tubes Mk II to fire 21in torpedoes. Originally intended to fire the Mk V torpedo, it was discovered during trials that the tubes were located too high above the waterline. The problems were initially resolved by strengthening the torpedo and changing the angle of entry into the water but the later ships adopted the Mk VII torpedo with its heavier warhead.

Dorsetshire in July 1930. The last pair were completed with a DCT and consequently the tall tower at the back of the bridge was omitted. (*Wright & Logan Collection*)

Some ships carried an aircraft even before a catapult was fitted, although operation was somewhat restricted since the seaplane had to be lowered into the sea for take-off. This is a Seagull III aboard HMAS *Australia*. The ship was eventually fitted with a catapult in September 1935.

Careers, Refits and Modifications

Berwick, *Cornwall, Cumberland, Kent, Suffolk* and *Dorsetshire* spent the majority of their pre-war careers on the China Station; *Australia* and *Canberra* in Australian waters; *Devonshire, London, Shropshire* and *Sussex* in the Mediterranean; and *Norfolk* in home waters and on the West and East Indies stations. They were involved in many exercises and those based overseas frequently took part in official visits.

Some points of interest during this period include:

In October 1929 *Cumberland* carried the Secretary of State for War and Parliamentary and Financial Secretaries of the Admiralty and their private secretaries from Gibraltar to Chatham. In August 1937, she and her sister *Suffolk* stood-by off the Putu Islands to assist in the defence of the Shanghai International Settlement, during which Chinese aircraft attacked Japanese shipping in the vicinity and two bombs near missed the *Cumberland*. In 1938 *Cumberland* carried the Commander-in-Chief on an inspection of his command, the first visit being to Singapore for the opening of the new base there on 14 February. In December 1928 *Kent* went to Yokohama to represent Great Britain at the Coronation Review of the Japanese Emperor Hirohito.

Australia carried out an exchange with her sister *Sussex* in 1935. *Canberra* visited the China Station in 1932 and acted as escort for HRH the Duke of Gloucester when he visited Australia in 1934.

Soon after joining the Mediterranean Fleet, *Devonshire* experienced an explosion, which killed 17 of the ship's company, in one of her 8in turrets during gunnery firings in the Aegean Sea. *London* took part in the Jubilee Review of July 1935 at Spithead and in non-intervention patrols during the Spanish Civil War. In August 1936 *Shropshire* acted as Refugee Control Ship at Barcelona.

During the war the 'County' class cruisers spent much of their time either as convoy escorts or on broader trade protection duties. Some highlights of their wartime careers are given under each ships' individual histories below.

During peacetime these cruisers underwent a number of 'regular' refits which did not greatly alter their capability or their appearance. The one exception was the addition of 'aircraft handling capabilities' which,

A close-up view of the aircraft arrangements on *Devonshire* in the mid 1930s. A Hawker Osprey seaplane K3633 is visible. The two-seat Osprey entered service in 1932 and was the RN's first fighter-reconnaissance aircraft. *(National Maritime Museum N20819)*

because of a perceived shortage of aircraft carriers, greatly interested the Admiralty and included the design of and experimentation with many different types of catapult. These aircraft facilities added considerable weight to the vessels but inclining experiments of the vessels as first built had shown that their displacement was well below the treaty limit and so the additional weight could be accommodated. They were completed with the support for a catapult, but no catapult, so some ships temporarily carried a floatplane that was lowered into the water for take-off. Various kinds of aircraft were envisaged for different cruiser roles, including two-seat fighter-reconnaissance and three-seat spotter-reconnaissance aircraft, so there were a number of catapult designs under development.

In April 1931 both *Dorsetshire* and *Norfolk* received one spotter-reconnaissance aircraft but no catapult. *Cornwall* initially received a light catapult Type SIIL (S stood for Slider – *ie* extendable); this was of Admiralty design, cordite operated, and capable of deploying a single-seat Fairey Flycatcher floatplane fighter. In 1932 *London* and *Sussex* also received a spotter-reconnaissance aircraft, again without a catapult. *Kent* (after a brief period with a FIL folding catapult), *Suffolk* and *Cumberland* were each given the same type of catapult as *Cornwall*. However, *Norfolk* and *Shropshire* received heavier EIIH catapults and a spotter-reconnaissance aircraft. By April 1933 *Berwick* had also received a light catapult, and *Dorsetshire, London, Devonshire, Sussex, Australia* and *Canberra* had received heavy catapults.

In the late 1930s four ships were rebuilt with hangars and a cross-deck catapult capable of handling a Walrus amphibian. There was still some concern that the cruisers as rebuilt might be overweight and so the first two vessels to receive a reconstruction, *Cumberland* and *Suffolk*, had the

Aircraft arrangements were so important that they were central to the late-1930s plans to reconstruct the 'Counties'. *Cumberland* in August 1936 following her refit clearly shows the large hangar for two Walrus aircraft and the transverse fixed DIH catapult that was the most visible alteration. The after single 4in HA have been replaced by twin 4in gun mountings, but the forward pair of singles remain. Her cut down quarterdeck is also visible. *(Wright & Logan Collection)*

The heavy EIIH catapult amidships in HMS *Norfolk* in September 1934. The aircraft is a Fairey IIIF, the standard three-seat spotter-reconnaissance aircraft of the time.

Berwick in 1932 wearing the buff and white livery of the China Station. Although no aircraft is visible, the canvas-covered catapult can just be made out abaft the third funnel.

quarterdeck cut down in height. Apart from *London*, which was completely reconstructed, the other ships were given heavy catapults and Walrus aircraft.

The additions just prior to and during World War II related primarily to enhancing AA protection and the addition of radar sensors. Some of the major changes are outlined in the individual ship histories below.

HMS *BERWICK*

Modifications. In spring 1930 *Berwick* was given the HACS 1 and a catapult, the catapult being replaced by a Type SIIL in 1932. Two quadruple 0.5in machine guns were also fitted to port and starboard of her foremast in 1932.

Berwick received a major refit/rebuild between July 1937 and November 1938, during which her bridge was modified and a heavier director was fitted. The after control platform was replaced by an aircraft hangar and two cranes for aircraft handling were fitted. She also had a narrow 5in belt of armour added at her waterline, behind the existing bulges. Her AA battery was increased by the fitting of four twin 4in AA guns in place of the original singles and the addition of two 8-barrelled pom-poms. Her torpedo tubes were removed.

Between February and April 1941 *Berwick* received a Type 286M modified RAF radar to provide a limited warning capability. Type 284 main armament fire control radar was also fitted, as were eleven single 20mm Oerlikon guns and the two quad 0.5in MGs were removed. Between May and September 1942, she had her hangar removed. A radar lantern for Type 273 was fitted on a lattice mast amidships

Berwick after the refit of 1937-38, with the new aircraft hangar obvious in this view. The cradle for the cross-deck catapult can also be seen. As yet the ship has not been fitted with the new DCT on the rebuilt bridge. Unlike the first two ships reconstructed in this way, the quarterdeck was not cut down. *(Seapower Centre via D Hobbs)*

and extra Oerlikon 20mm AA guns were fitted on 'B' and 'X' turrets. Four fire control radars Type 283 were fitted to provide the main armament with AA barrage control. In the autumn of 1943 she again underwent a refit, her close range AA armament then being two 8-barrelled 2pdr pom-poms, seven twin and two single 20mm Oerlikons; two more single 20mm were added in 1944.

Wartime highlights. On completion of her reconstruction, *Berwick* re-commissioned for service in the West Indies and became flagship of 8th Cruiser Squadron based at Bermuda, where after the outbreak of war she spent much of her time searching for commerce raiders. After a refit she transferred to the 1st Cruiser Squadron, Home Fleet, and on 2 March 1940 she intercepted and boarded the German freighter *Wolfsburg* which was on fire, eventually sinking the freighter by gunfire. Three days later, she again intercepted and boarded another German freighter, this time the *Uruguay*, which had also been set on fire by her crew and had to be sunk by gunfire.

In April *Berwick* was recalled to support the planned landings in Norway (Operation R4), and on 3 April she embarked soldiers of the Royal Lincolnshire Regiment at Rosyth, putting them ashore in Norway five days later. With other cruisers, she sailed from Rosyth and was joined by a French cruiser and two destroyers off Kinnaird Head, and they all participated in a sweep to the north east.

On completion of this, *Berwick* joined the battleships *Rodney*, *Valiant* and *Warspite*, and the aircraft carrier *Furious*. *Berwick* and the ships in company came under heavy and sustained German air attacks, during which the destroyer *Gurkha* was sunk. *Berwick* was deployed as escort for *Furious* during the air attacks on Trondheim and then joined other ships to carry out a search of the Trondheim Leads for German troopships. The search included Aandsfjord and Vaagsfjord and in the middle of the month *Berwick* rejoined the Home Fleet ships off North Cape, where she was near missed during air attacks without significant damage.

During April *Berwick* also acted as escort for the aircraft carriers *Ark Royal* and *Furious* on their passage to the Norwegian coast for air operations (Operation DX). The beginning of May found *Berwick* under air attack off Norway during the continuation of Operation DX. She then joined ships in the Clyde and embarked an advance party of Royal Marines for passage to Iceland (Operation Fork). The marines were landed on the 10th at Reykjavik and the fjords were searched for enemy activity. German nationals were embarked for passage to Great Britain for detention. Shortly after completing a refit, *Berwick* sustained damage in a collision with a merchant ship on 4 August.

Berwick took passage from the Clyde, with the battleship *Barham*, to join the Fleet in the Mediterranean (Operation Coat). They arrived at Gibraltar on 6 November and the next day sailed with Force F to join ships of Force H for escort duties during the passage to land stores and personnel in Malta. The convoy came under air attack, but the expected submarine threat failed to materialise. On the 10th she disembarked troops and stores in Malta and then took passage to join the other Mediterranean Fleet ships, her first task being to provide cover during the air attacks from the aircraft carrier *Illustrious* on the Italian fleet at Taranto (Operation Judgement). On arrival at Alexandria, on the 14th, *Berwick* joined the 3rd Cruiser Squadron and then embarked troops for passage to Piraeus.

Later in the month, *Berwick* sailed to Malta, along with the battleship *Ramillies* and the cruiser *Newcastle* (Operation Collar). This operation was carried out in conjunction with Force H and included the transfer of ships to Gibraltar covered by the battleships *Barham* and *Malaya*, and the aircraft carrier *Eagle*. On 27 November *Berwick* met the battlecruiser *Renown*, the cruiser *Sheffield* and the aircraft carrier *Ark Royal* and took part in the surface action against Italian Fleet units known as the Battle of Spartivento, when she was hit by two 8in shells and sustained damage to her after turret.

On completion of repairs at Gibraltar, *Berwick* resumed convoy escort duties and, at dawn on Christmas Day the convoy

Berwick in November 1945. The most visible difference from earlier views is the after superstructure which replaced the hangar at the end of 1942. The ship still carries the late-war colour scheme camouflage pattern. *(Wright & Logan Collection)*

The bridge of *Cornwall* as completed. The ships were intended to carry a new fire control system, but the large DCT which was part of the system was still under development when the ships were designed. Instead, at the back of the bridge they were fitted with a large square windowed tower with all-round visibility that housed the spotters and plotting area, topped with a small rangefinder-director. This ruined the aerodynamics of the bridge, creating troublesome draughts for watchkeeping personnel.

came under attack by the German cruiser *Admiral Hipper* and was scattered. *Berwick* engaged the German ship and was hit by four shells, causing damage to the after superstructure and gun mountings. The wounded were landed at Gibraltar, where *Berwick* received temporary repairs to enable her to return to Great Britain for permanent repairs, which lasted for the majority of 1941. November 1941 found *Berwick* deployed as an escort for the battleship *Duke of York* and two days later (together with her sister ships *Kent* and *Suffolk*) as an escort for the battleship *King George V* and the aircraft carrier *Victorious* which were on passage to Iceland after a report of a possible break-out into the Atlantic by the German battleships *Admiral Scheer* and *Tirpitz*.

On 4 March 1942 she sailed with the battleship *King George V*, the aircraft carrier *Victorious* and a number of destroyers to join the battleships *Duke of York* and *Renown* which were acting as part of the cover for Russian convoys. With the continuing threat of *Tirpitz*, *Berwick* continued with patrol duties until arrangements were made to deal with machinery problems at Devonport. During July, she took passage from Iceland with her sister *Norfolk* to join Home Fleet units for a diversionary operation off the Norwegian coast (Operation Camera); 1943 was mainly spent on convoy escort duties and undergoing a refit.

During March and April 1944 *Berwick* carried out preparations for the forthcoming landings in Normandy. After escorting the aircraft carriers *Furious* and *Searcher* during air strikes on coastal shipping in the Kristiansund North area (Operation Croquet) during May, *Berwick*, together with other ships of the Home Fleet, provided cover for the Normandy landings against any interference by German surface ships (Operation Neptune). She was also involved in Operation Lombard, part of the deception plans for Neptune.

Throughout July and August *Berwick*

was deployed with the Home Fleet carrying out various operations off Norway, including unsuccessful air attacks on *Tirpitz* by aircraft from the carriers *Indefatigable*, *Formidable*, *Furious*, *Nabob* and *Trumpeter* (Operation Goodwood). At the beginning of September, she was deployed with her sisters *Kent* and *Devonshire* to escort the RMS *Queen Mary* during her Atlantic passage taking the Prime Minister and Defence Staff to Canada for a meeting with the US President (Operation Octagon). After spending some time at Scapa Flow, these same cruisers provided the escort for the return voyage of the *Queen Mary* and her valuable 'cargo'.

In the middle of May 1945 *Berwick* was involved in the arrangements for the collection of U-boats for passage from Norway to Great Britain and, at the end of the month, together with her sister *Norfolk*, was employed transporting military personnel and stores to Norway and Iceland, returning to Portsmouth in June. Here she prepared for trooping duties, on completion of which she was reduced to reserve at Portsmouth, eventually being sold in the middle of 1948.

HMS *CORNWALL*

Modifications. *Cornwall* received HACS 1 in 1929/30 and a catapult Type SIIL in 1930/31; later two quad 0.5in MGs were added abreast the foremast. During her major refit in 1936/37, the eight 21in torpedo tubes were removed to make room for a large hangar which could accommodate two Walrus amphibious aircraft, the single 4in AA mounts were replaced by twin Mk XIX mountings and multiple pom-poms Mk VI were fitted in lieu of the single mounts. In February 1941 her AA armament was improved by the addition of 20mm weapons.

Wartime highlights. *Cornwall* was serving on the China Station when war broke out and soon transferred to the East Indies Station where she operated primarily from Colombo. On 10 October she was sent on an unsuccessful search for the German pocket battleship *Admiral Graf Spee* in the area south of Ceylon; 1940 was spent operating from South Africa apart from a short period under repair in Liverpool.

At the beginning of September she supported the landings by Free French troops at Dakar (Operation Menace) and then took part in a search for a Vichy French warship which was on passage from Dakar to Gabon, French Guinea. On the 19th *Cornwall*, together with the cruiser *Delhi*, intercepted the cruiser *Primaguet* and the tanker *Tarn* in the Gulf of Guinea. These two vessels returned to Casablanca rather than face a naval engagement, escorted by the British cruisers.

In May 1941 *Cornwall* sank the German raider *Pinguin*, which had pretended to be a

Norwegian vessel when intercepted after she had sunk the tanker *British Premier*. A number of the crew of the *Pinguin* were rescued, along with 22 prisoners from captured ships.

In early April 1942 *Cornwall* joined the battleship *Warspite*, the aircraft carriers *Formidable* and *Indomitable*, and the cruisers *Enterprise*, *Emerald* and her sister *Dorsetshire* in an unsuccessful search for a Japanese naval force reported on passage toward Ceylon. She was detached, with her sister *Dorsetshire*, to escort the military convoy SU4 and then recalled after the Japanese warships were sighted. The two cruisers were themselves sighted during their return passage by aircraft from the Japanese cruiser *Tone* and they came under heavy attack by dive-bombers from the aircraft carriers *Akagi*, *Soryu* and *Hiryu* on the 5th. *Cornwall* was quickly disabled and sunk within 15 minutes, with heavy casualties, including 190 killed or missing. *Dorsetshire* was sunk by similar attacks some 6 minutes later; 1122 survivors from the two cruisers were rescued.

HMS *CUMBERLAND*

Modifications. *Cumberland* was given the same aircraft facilities as *Cornwall*, the catapult being fitted whilst on the China Station. She was the first of the class to receive a major refit (February 1935 to July 1936), during which the catapult was replaced by the heavier Type DIH and a large hangar was installed. The two after 4in AA mountings were replaced by twins. She underwent a further refit in 1938, when her anti-aircraft armament was further enhanced, with her forward single 4in AA guns also being replaced by twin mountings, and two quadruple 2pdrs fitted port and starboard of her fore funnel. Two quadruple 0.5in machine guns were also fitted on her hangar roof and her original four single 2pdr guns were removed. During the second half of 1941 tripod masts replaced her original pole masts, and four single 20mm guns were added (increased to seven in 1942). Extra radar was also mounted and shelter facilities were provided for the 4in guns' crews.

A close-up of *Cornwall* in 1938, showing details of the recently completed reconstruction. Apart from the addition of the large hangar, the bridge was rearranged and reduced in height, with the new DCT on top. The 4in singles have been replaced by twins, and note the position of the forward mounting abreast the foremast. *(National Maritime Museum N8279)*

Cumberland was the prototype for the major reconstruction planned for the *Kent* class. Concerns about weight breaching treaty limits led to the cutting down of the quarterdeck by one deck, which also applied to *Suffolk* but not the later modified ships; also only the aftermost 4in mounts were replaced by twins. The bridge also underwent less alteration than later ships. *(Naval Photograph Club)*

A revealing overhead photograph of *Cumberland* in 1942, with light AA positions on B and X turret and the hangar roof. The ship still carries the aircraft facilities (removed in 1943) and the Walrus amidships is shown being deployed with wings partially folded. *(Via Dimi Apostolopoulos)*

In 1943 *Cumberland* received a refit prior to being transferred to the Eastern Fleet. The aircraft facilities (hangar and catapult) were removed and changes made to the radar equipment including the installation of surface warning radar Type 273, fire control radar Type 285 for the forward 4in HA armament and air warning radar Type 281 with an IFF interrogator outfit. Close range fire control radar Type 282 was also fitted. On completion of this refit, her AA armament comprised four twin 4in, two quadruple 2pdrs and five twin and four single 20mm guns. In another refit from January to March 1945, she was fitted with two extra single 20mm guns.

Cumberland was refitted at Devonport between 1949 and 1951, in order to undertake the role of a trials cruiser, when lattice masts, new directors and added accommodation (larger superstructures) were provided. The original armament was entirely removed and she emerged initially (April 1951) with a twin 4in and a twin 40mm gun on her port side and a single 4.5in gun on her starboard side. In 1955 she visited the Mediterranean to try a new twin 3in gun, which was fitted in 'X' position. In May 1956 she sailed for the Mediterranean again for more trials with the 3in gun and the new automatic twin 6in Mk 26 gun, mounted in 'B' position. An MRS3 director was mounted on her bridge to control the guns. The 6in and 3in gun mountings were the prototypes for the automatic guns to be fitted in the new *Tiger* class cruisers.

Wartime highlights. At the beginning of the war *Cumberland* joined the South American Division of the 8th Cruiser Squadron and, following the report of an aircraft sighting of the German pocket battleship *Admiral Graf Spee* and the tanker *Altmark*, she moved to Rio de Janeiro, but the enemy ships escaped interception. However on 5 December *Cumberland* was involved, with the cruiser *Ajax*, in the interception of the German ship *Ussukuma*, which scuttled herself. Following self-refit and boiler cleaning at Port Stanley, *Cumberland* was ordered to join *Exeter*, *Ajax* and *Achilles* off the Plate estuary after the *Graf Spee* had sought refuge in Montevideo following her defeat in Battle of the River Plate. She arrived on 14 December and, after *Graf Spee* scuttled herself, returned to Port Stanley.

In September 1940 *Cumberland* joined the aircraft carrier *Ark Royal*, the battleships *Resolution* and *Barham*, and her sister ships *Devonshire* and *Australia* in support of the Free French landing at Dakar (Operation Menace). Whilst there she provided naval gunfire support and was hit by a 9.4in shell from a shore battery which fractured a steam pipe causing the loss of electrical power and so *Cumberland* was withdrawn from the operation and returned to Freetown at the end of the month. The first part of 1941 was spent in the

A photo dated 21 February 1942 shows *Cumberland* with tripod masts. Zarebas for additional light AA guns have been added on X turret and the after corners of the hangar roof, but as yet they are still empty. The ship is painted in a four-colour camouflage scheme.

Cumberland as a trials ship in May 1956. She is carrying prototypes of the twin 6in (forward) and twin 3in (aft) that were later fitted to the *Tiger* class cruisers.

Atlantic followed by a refit in Great Britain.

In January 1942 *Cumberland* took passage to Murmansk and embarked the Foreign Secretary, Sir Stafford Cripps, for the return passage to Great Britain as part of convoy QP5. At the end of June, she formed part of a force (together with the battleship *Duke of York*, the US battleship *Washington*, the cruiser *Nigeria* and a screen of fourteen RN and USN destroyers) to cover the passage of convoy PQ17. At the end of October, she sailed from Scapa Flow with her sister *Norfolk* and a screen of five destroyers to support the allied landings in North Africa (Operation Torch). The year 1943 was spent on convoy escort duties and undergoing a refit on the Tyne.

Cumberland transferred to Ceylon via the Mediterranean, with her sister *London*, in January 1944. Her first offensive sweep in the Indian Ocean as part of the 4th Cruiser Squadron, with the battleships *Queen Elizabeth*, *Valiant* and *Renown*, the aircraft carrier *Illustrious* and the cruisers *London*, *Gambia* and *Ceylon* (Operation Diplomat), took place on 21 March. Later that month she joined with the US TG58.5 off the Cocos Islands and transferred to the 5th Cruiser Squadron of the Eastern Fleet at the beginning of June. In July *Cumberland* joined with the Eastern Fleet in offensive operation against targets in Sumatra with the battleships *Queen Elizabeth*, *Valiant* and *Renown*, the French battleship *Richelieu* and the cruisers *Nigeria*, *Kenya*, *Ceylon* and *Gambia* (Operation Crimson), including the bombardment of Sabang on the 25th of the month.

After taking part in air operations with the aircraft carriers *Victorious* and *Indomitable* attacking Sigli in Northern Sumatra (Operation Light), *Cumberland*, together with her sisters *London* and *Suffolk*, bombarded airfields on the Nicobar Islands, an operation intended to provide a diversion for the US assault on Leyte. In April 1945 *Cumberland* joined TG63.2 with the battleship *Queen Elizabeth*, the French battleship *Richelieu* and her sister *London* to cover air reconnaissance flights from the escort carriers *Empress* and *Khedive* at Port Swettenham and Port Dickson, Malaya (Operation Sunfish). Bombardments of various targets in the area followed before

Cumberland briefly joined TF68 at the beginning of May, later that month transferring to TF61 for Operations Dukedom and Mitre.

In August *Cumberland* was involved in the support of military operations in Malaya (Operation Zipper). At the end of the month she was deployed in the Indian Ocean off Sumatra to assist in military operations after the Japanese surrender, eventually arriving in Singapore at the beginning of September. She returned to Great Britain in November 1945 and spent some time under repair at Chatham before undertaking trooping duties from the Far East, which lasted until June 1946. For the rest of her service she was used as a trials cruiser after conversion at Devonport, which was completed in May 1951, and was placed in reserve in May 1959, being broken up later that year.

HMS *KENT*

Modifications. HACS and a light catapult Type FIL (later replaced by a SIIL) were fitted around 1930. Small enhancements were later made to her AA capability (two single 4in guns added and two quad 0.5in MGs). As completed, *Kent* was slightly heavier than her sisters and so did not receive a hangar or the heavy cross-deck catapult in her version of the major reconstruction in 1937/38: the single 4in gun mountings were replaced by four twin 4in mountings; two 8-barrelled 2pdr pom-pom AA guns were fitted either side of the superstructure and the AA defence was enhanced by the fitting of High Angle Control Directors in place of rangefinders. The after superstructure was replaced by a lattice searchlight tower, with the 8in director relocated abaft, and the bridge was rearranged and a DCT fitted. Although there was no hangar, the SIIL was replaced by a heavy EIVH catapult capable of launching a Walrus amphibian, handled by two cranes, one each either side of the after funnel. A narrow belt of armour plate was fitted at waterline level over the machinery spaces and the torpedo tube mountings were removed.

In 1941 six 20mm Oerlikon guns were fitted on the turrets and the after superstructure. Radar Type 284 for fire control of the forward main armament mountings was

Kent in August 1930 fitted with one of the early lightweight catapults, capable only of launching a single-seat fighter like the Fairey Flycatcher, clearly shown abaft the funnels. *(Wright & Logan Collection)*

fitted and radar Type 285 for the fire control of the secondary AA armament. Radar Type 281 was also fitted, for aircraft warning.

In 1942 a surface warning centimetric radar Type 273 was fitted aft on the searchlight tower. Six more single 20mm Oerlikon guns were fitted to improve close range AA defence. Another refit occurred in September 1943, when four radars Type 283 were fitted to provide barrage control for the 4in AA directors; three twin 20mm were added and six singles removed.

Wartime highlights. Following a period initially based at Hong Kong and then at Colombo and escort duties in the Indian Ocean, in May 1940 *Kent* transferred to the 3rd Cruiser Squadron for service with the Mediterranean Fleet. Later in the month she covered the transit of the battleship *Valiant*, the aircraft carrier *Illustrious* and the cruisers *Calcutta* and *Coventry* during their passage to reinforce the fleet at Alexandria (Operation Hats). In September she sailed with the battleship *Valiant* to provide cover during attacks from the aircraft carrier *Illustrious* and for the bombardment of Bardia. *Kent* was hit by a torpedo from an Italian aircraft on the 17th of the month and taken in tow by the destroyer *Nubian*. Later she was able to proceed independently to Alexandria and then took passage to Simonstown for temporary repairs at the end of the month, before returning to Great Britain for permanent repairs.

At the beginning of November 1941 she sailed from Scapa Flow, with the battleship *King George V*, her sisters *Berwick* and *Suffolk* and the aircraft carrier *Victorious*, in search of the German warships *Admiral Scheer* and *Tirpitz*. After various convoy duties and a refit, in December 1942 *Kent* joined her sister *Berwick* as part of the

cover for the passage of return convoy RA51 from Kola Inlet. In January 1943 she once again formed part of the cover for a convoy, this time convoy JW52. Whilst carrying out this duty she came under unsuccessful air and U-boat attacks. After her arrival at Kola Inlet, almost immediately she joined the cruisers *Bermuda* and *Glasgow* for the return convoy RA52.

At the beginning of July 1943 *Kent* formed part of a diversion for the allied landings in Sicily (Operation Camera) by operating off the coast of Norway. In August she went to Halifax, Nova Scotia in order to form part of the escort for the battlecruiser *Renown* which was to take the Prime Minister back to the Clyde after the Quadrant Conference with the US President at Quebec, entering a month long refit at Chatham on her return. After post-refit trials *Kent* remained with the Home Fleet based at Scapa Flow during the Normandy landings in June 1944 (Operation Neptune) to provide distant cover in the event of any attempt by major German warships to interfere with this operation.

Later in the year she provided cover, together with the battleship *Duke of York*, her sister *Devonshire* and the cruisers *Jamaica* and *Bellona*, for the unsuccessful air attacks on the German battleship *Tirpitz* in Altenfjord, Norway (Operation Mascot) by aircraft from the aircraft carriers *Formidable*, *Furious* and *Victorious*. After providing cover during air operations by the aircraft carriers *Indefatigable*, *Trumpeter* and *Nabob* on airfields at Goosen, Norway, *Kent* escorted the aircraft carriers *Nabob* and *Trumpeter* during further unsuccessful air strikes on the German battleship *Tirpitz*. At the beginning of September, she escorted, together with her sisters *Devonshire* and *Berwick*, RMS *Queen Mary* during a passage of the Atlantic when she was

taking the Prime Minister to attend the Octagon Conference with the US President.

In February 1945 *Kent* was placed in Category B reserve and at 4 months notice for return to operational use and remained as such until placed on the disposal list in 1947. She was sold in January 1948 and broken up later that year.

HMS *SUFFOLK*

Modifications. Having received the usual aircraft arrangements in 1931, *Suffolk* underwent a major refit between August 1935 and October 1936, as for *Cumberland*, except for a new model of single 4in gun, with a shield, replacing two of the original version (the other two were replaced by twin Mk XIX). In September 1939 a pre-production air warning radar outfit Type 79Z was fitted. In 1940/41, she was under repair, which included the installation of a surface gunnery control radar, Type 284, and replacement of the air warning radar fitted in 1939 by the production Type 279. Fire control radar Type 284 was fitted for control of the main armament and Type 285 radar for the control of secondary armament. Twin 4in mountings were fitted in place of the single mountings, and six 20mm Oerlikons added.

In 1942 *Suffolk* received a refit, during which the radar Type 279 was replaced by a new design Type 281. The centimetric radar Type 273, also of new design, was fitted to provide surface warning. Six more 20mm Oerlikon guns were fitted for close range defence.

In early 1943 radar Type 282 was fitted for fire control of the close range AA defence. At that time, the close range 20mm armament comprised five twin and three single mountings.

Wartime highlights. After she had joined the 1st Cruiser Squadron in the Mediterranean, the squadron was recalled to Great Britain and so *Suffolk* returned in November, with her sister *Devonshire*. On 23 November she joined the search for the German battleships *Scharnhorst* and *Gneisenau* after the Armed Merchant Cruiser *Rawalpindi* had been sunk. In early February 1940 *Suffolk* sustained some damage in a collision with the SS *Misram* and did not rejoin her squadron until April. Later in the month she landed some Royal Marines for the initial occupation of the Faeroe Islands (Operation Valentine), and then joined her sisters *Devonshire* and *Berwick* for the support of military operations in Norway. During her passage she intercepted the German tanker *Skagerrak* which scuttled herself on *Suffolk*'s approach. Whilst bombarding Stavanger airfield (Operation Duck) in the middle of the month, she came under heavy air attack for several hours. *Suffolk* only received one direct hit but this, and

Kent did not receive a surface search radar until her refit of July –November 1942, the lantern for which (Type 273) can be seen on the lattice tower aft. At the same time the catapult was removed and a further six 20mm Oerlikons added.

Amidships details of *Suffolk* in February 1937. Careful inspection shows the single 4in shielded mount forward of the standard Mk XIX twin. *Suffolk* was the only ship of the class to carry this single mounting, but it was replaced by a twin in 1941. *(Wright & Logan Collection)*

Suffolk in 1937 after her refit clearly shows the hangar, with its twin roller doors, and cut-down quarterdeck.

An aerial view of Suffolk in August 1941 with a Walrus on the catapult. A few months earlier the ship had scored a notable success for radar by tracking Bismarck for a day and a half

the numerous near misses, caused major damage aft that disabled the steering gear and resulted in extensive flooding and fires, reducing her speed to 18 knots. Steering by engines and with her quarterdeck awash, *Suffolk* returned to Scapa Flow for temporary repairs before receiving permanent repairs at Greenock, a job which lasted until she rejoined her squadron at Scapa Flow in March 1941.

Following the initial sighting of the German battleship *Bismarck* on 23 May, together with her sister *Norfolk*, she shadowed *Bismarck* and her consort *Prinz Eugen* until the enemy ships were engaged by the battlecruiser *Hood* and the battleship *Prince of Wales*. Using radar, the cruisers initially remained in contact with the enemy ships after the loss of *Hood* but, after losing contact, *Suffolk* was detached to Iceland to refuel, finally returning to Scapa Flow at the end of June and being present at the royal visit by His Majesty King George VI.

November 1941 to February 1942 found *Suffolk* employed on attempts to intercept the German battleships *Tirpitz* and *Admiral Scheer*, which were reported as attempting to break out into the Atlantic. At the begin-

ning of 1943 *Suffolk* underwent a refit and spent the remainder of the year and the beginning of 1944 on various convoy duties. In March, with the destroyer *Quadrant*, she took part in a search for U-boat supply ship *Brake* (Operation Covered). Following a refit at Durban she joined the 5th Cruiser Squadron, Eastern Fleet at Ceylon, where she formed part of TF63. In the middle of October she formed part of TG63.2, with her sisters *Cumberland* and *London*, for a diversionary operation against Japanese targets on the Nicobar Islands during the US landings on Leyte (Operation Millet).

On 1 January 1945 *Suffolk* was deployed, with the cruisers *Ceylon*, *Argonaut* and *Black Prince*, as part of TF65 to cover air attacks by aircraft from the aircraft carriers *Indomitable*, *Victorious* and *Indefatigable* on oil refineries at Pangkalan Brandan, Sumatra (Operation Lentil). She also formed part of the escort of the liner carrying HRH The Duke of Gloucester (Governor General designate of Australia) during the final leg of his journey from Fremantle to Sydney. In March *Suffolk* supported military operations in Burma and was based at Akyab, where she assisted in temporary repair of the destroyer *Rapid*.

April saw further deployment in the Malacca Strait and off the Burmese coast, ending the month as part of a large force intended to prevent interference by Japanese warships during the British landings near Rangoon (Operation Dracula) and providing cover during air strikes on airfields and bombardment of shore targets at Car Nicobar and Port Blair. At the beginning of May she formed part of TF63, which was providing cover for landing operations. After further escort duties, *Suffolk* was withdrawn from operational fleet duty in July and returned to Great Britain for trooping duties.

Suffolk was used to bring repatriated military and civil personnel from Australia until late May 1946. In July she was reduced to reserve status at Chatham and sold in 1948, breaking up being completed by January 1949.

Continued on p.49

Model Products

EAGLEWALL   1:1200 scale

The British company of Eaglewall manufactured two plastic kits of the 'County' class cruisers for their 'Battle' series – HMS *Dorsetshire* and HMS *Norfolk*. These could be built as waterline or as full-hull models and the artwork on the box tops was particularly exciting for the younger modellers. The kits were accurate and are still much sought after, long after production ceased.

Far left: The exciting box top artwork of HMS *Dorsetshire*.

Left: This picture of HMS *Norfolk* shows the cleanly moulded components of these much sought after kits.

AIRFIX   1:1200 scale

Airfix released just one plastic model of this class in 1976 – a smaller scale version of their standard series 1:600 scale kit of HMS *Suffolk*. This was to be the last release in their short-lived 1:1200 scale series and was available for just a few years, but in 2011 it was re-released, forming part of a 'Sink The Bismarck!' set and, as the title suggests, was sold along with six other models, the majority of which had been released in the past as separate kits.

As with others in this series, it was a waterline model with a one-piece hull and separate deck moulding. The main superstructure was another moulding with the bridge being supplied in two parts. The gun mountings were moulded with integral barrels. The aircraft cranes and boats were supplied as single-piece mouldings, but no davits were provided. The three funnels were each moulded in two halves.

The kits were sold in a clear plastic bubble packaging on a card back. The assembly instructions, provided in the form of four simple diagrams, were printed on the reverse of the card.

Left: The packaging of HMS *Suffolk* clearly displays the components of the kit to the purchaser.

NAVIS/NEPTUN   1:1250 scale

Navis/Neptun produce five models – 1132 HMS *Norfolk* (1941), 1133 HMS *Sussex* (1942), 1133a HMS *London* (1941), 1134a HMS *Suffolk* (1942) and 1134b HMS

Right: The detailed model of HMS *Norfolk* with a case to protect the very fine rigging.

Above: The basic model of HMS *Sussex*.

Above: HMS *Suffolk* by XP Forge; note the oversize masts.

Right: The two boxes portraying HMAS *Australia* and HMAS *Canberra*.

Above: The major components contained in the kit for HMAS *Australia*.

Berwick (1941). The latter two clearly show the aircraft hangar that was added and have some boats deployed on their davits. The differences in appearance when compared to the first two are most notice-

able. The basic models are painted overall grey with just a few colour highlights (*eg* funnel tops) but more detailed models, complete with more enhanced painting and rigging are also available, although only HMS *Norfolk* is available in this form.

XP FORGE
1:1200 scale

This American company produces a one-piece model of HMS *Sussex*. Being

just one-piece, the turrets do not rotate and the model simply requires painting. No colour details are given, nor any other information at all. The model demonstrates the characteristics of the class, but it is simplified, and the masts are grossly oversize.

This one-piece model is really for the wargamer, and not the collector.

B-RESINA
1:700 scale

The kit of HMS *Suffolk* (no longer in production) was dimensionally accurate but, like many B-Resina kits, based closely on the plastic Airfix 1:600 scale kit of the same subject and included many of the same errors. White metal was used for many of the smaller components, including the Walrus amphibian and the masts.

There was no photoetch. One significant error was with the three funnels which were located too close to each other and raked at too steep an angle. This was a simple model to assemble but one which needed significant work and much more detail to produce a truly accurate representation.

COMBRIG
1:700 scale

The kits from Combrig of the two Australian vessels are very similar, the main hull mouldings being identical. The vessels are depicted at different stages in their careers, HMAS *Canberra* being modelled with her original AA armament of just four single guns whilst HMAS *Australia* has four twin mountings. The differences in superstructure and other details are also modelled; the larger items were moulded separately with the smaller items being provided on a thin wafer.

The funnels, turrets, boats and other details all have very large resin 'pours' which need removal, rather surprisingly considering the very thin wafer carrying the smaller components. The gun barrels of the primary armament are moulded separately, and lengths of resin rod are supplied for the masts. Resin davits are also included, and

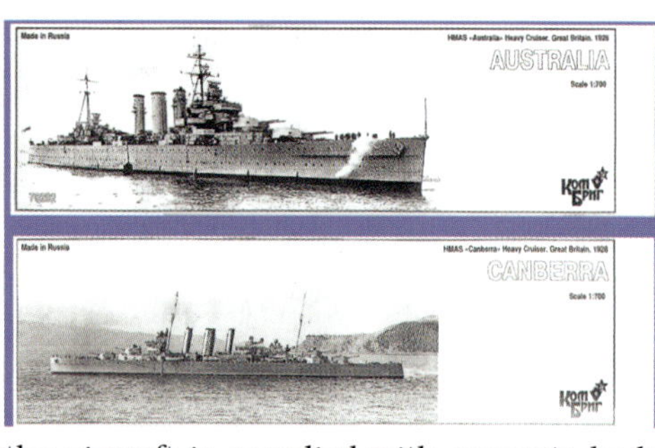

the aircraft is supplied with separate body and wings.

The aircraft catapult and cranes all carry clear indication of the struts but, being resin, are moulded as solid objects. No photoetch is included, and this is one particular area where it would be a great improvement. There are no painting details given and the instructions simply comprise images of the components and just one isometric assembly diagram. The written instructions are in Russian and appear to give some technical details and just a short history of the vessel.

The models are supplied in flimsy cardboard boxes with lumps of polystyrene to protect the components, which come in a plastic bag. This, unfortunately, frequently results in damage to the finer components.

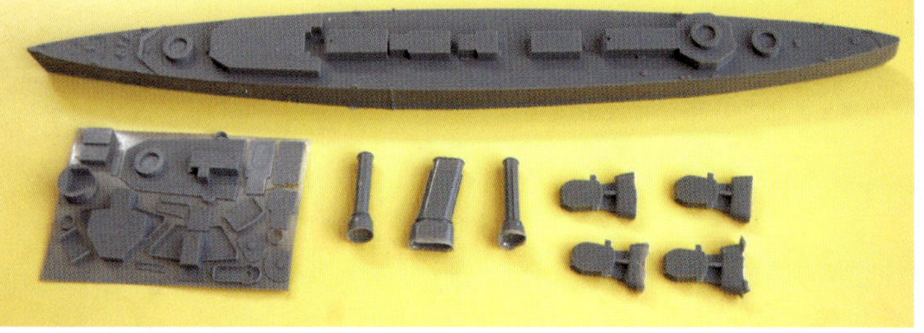

HI-MOLD

1:700 scale

The two Hi-Mold kits of HMS *Sussex* and HMS *Dorsetshire* (no longer in production) were accurate representations and included a small sheet of photoetch, brass gun barrels for the primary armament, with many of the smaller components in white metal. The instructions were in Japanese.

Left: The box of the HMS *Sussex* kit.

HP MODELS

1:700 scale

HP Models produced kits of HMS *Kent* (1941/42), HMS *Suffolk* (1942), HMS *Sussex* (1942), HMS *Norfolk* (1934), HMS *Berwick* (1943) and HMS *London* (1942). The differences in ship's appearance are well represented, this being particularly noticeable with the kit of HMS *London*, which portrays her as radically re-built with just two funnels.

Like all HP kits, these were waterline models. Quite a lot of detail was moulded onto the resin hull which required some careful painting and the scuttles needed to be drilled out as their locations were only indicated by very small holes, not much more than pin-pricks.

The three funnels were moulded separately but the details, including some relatively large parts of the superstructure, were moulded on very thin wafers, four large ones and several smaller ones. The 8in gun barrels were provided in turned brass (except for HMS *Sussex* which was released before the others) and there was a small sheet of flags – white ensigns, blue

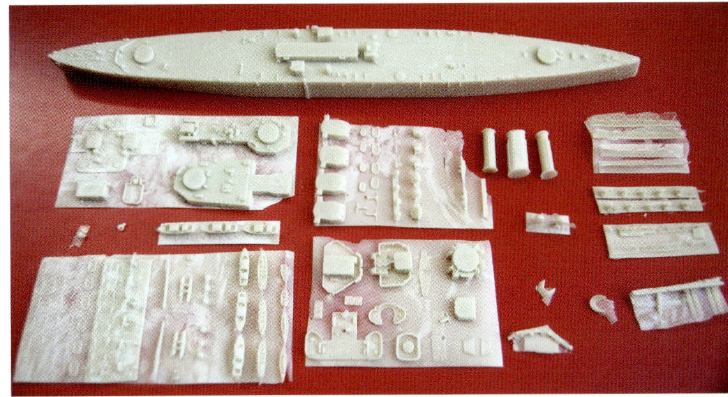

ensigns of the Royal Naval Reserve, union jacks and admiral's pennants. No rod was provided for the masts but detailed dimensions (both length and diameter) were given in the instructions.

The instructions comprised three further sheets – a line drawing of the cruiser, an overall assembly diagram and a sheet depicting the various components. There were no painting instructions or photoetch.

Above: The resin components of the kit for HMS *Dorsetshire*.

Below: Four of the boxes containing the HP Models kits. The different style of artwork for HMS *Sussex* betrays the earlier release of this version.

WHITE ENSIGN MODELS

1:700 scale

The White Ensign Models kit of HMS *Sussex* (1942) comprised a resin waterline hull, large resin mouldings for major parts of the superstructure and small ones for small details, a sheet of photoetch and some rod. Some small details were moulded onto the hull and the positions of the scuttles were indicated but required drilling. The larger superstructure mouldings followed a similar pattern but included substantial 'pours' which required removal. Most of the smaller components also included 'pours' but there was very little flash to be found.

The photoetch sheet included railings, a crane, radar tower, catapult, funnel cap grilles and many smaller parts for the masts

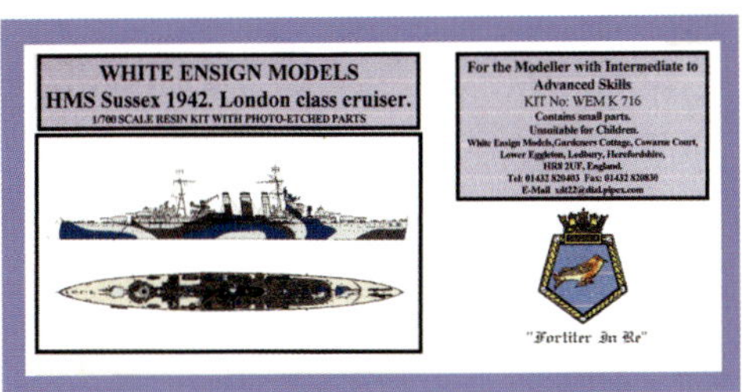

Left: The box for the kit of HMS *Sussex* includes a small representation of the camouflage pattern.

and other areas. Both brass and plastic rod was provided for the masts, for which detailed dimensions were given in the instructions. WEM suggested that modellers use brass in lieu of the plastic rod – provided they can find sufficiently fine material (0.010in diameter). The gun barrels for the 8in guns were provided in resin.

The instructions also included line drawings of the ship and an isometric assembly diagram, both showing the loca-tion of the components. When used in conjunction with the written instructions, there was little room for mistakes. A colour diagram showed the camouflage scheme worn by *Sussex* in 1942. The colours (light and dark grey and blue) were specified using Admiralty nomenclature and could all be found in WEM's own ColourCoats range of paints. Following the closure of WEM in the UK, these paints are now available from Resolution Hobbies

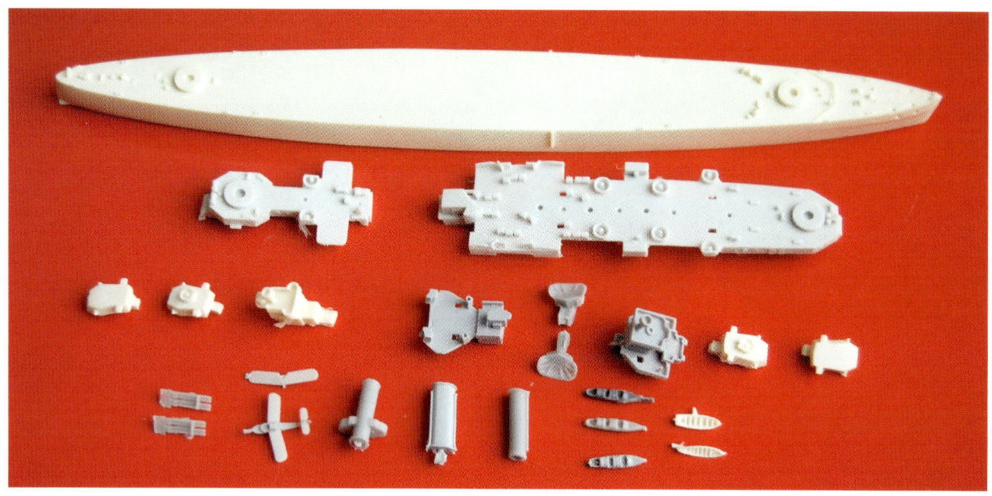

Right: The resin mouldings from the kit of HMS *Sussex*.

ATLANTIC MODELS

1:700 scale

Following the closure of WEM in the UK, Peter Hall of Atlantic Models, who had created the 'masters' for the WEM models, released a model of HMS *London* (1941). Not surprisingly, this was produced in a very similar format to the WEM model but did also include some 3D printed parts for the smaller calibre guns.

Instructions were provided in a 10-page

A4 colour booklet, which included painting details and a general arrangement drawing. The kit included some parts for the 1943 configuration, but details of their locations were not included.

Both the White Ensign and Atlantic Models kits have not been in production for some years, but are still eagerly sought after because of their accuracy and quality.

Right: The box for the kit of HMS *London* includes a photograph showing the camouflage pattern.

Below: The resin mouldings from the kit of HMS *London*.

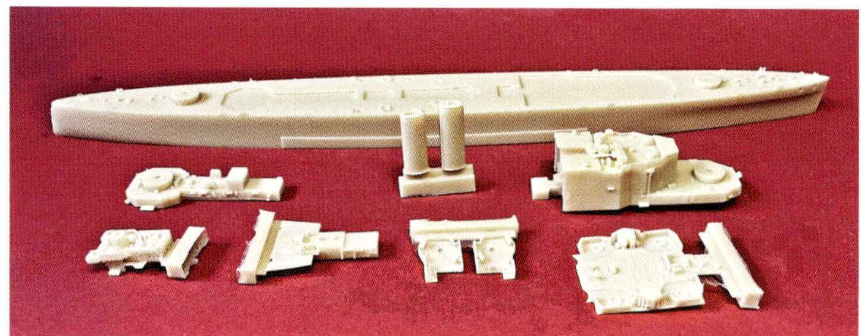

NT-MODEL

1:700 scale

NT-Model produce a 3D printed *Kent* class heavy cruiser white kit. The model is supplied in a robust plastic box for protection and comprises a one-piece hull and upperworks with separate masts, primary gun turrets, boats (some of which are suspended from davits), aircraft and catapult, and crane. There are no instruc-tions.

The masts are curved and many modellers will prefer to replace them with brass rod. The model appears to represent *Kent* in the early 1930s, with single 4in AA guns. The representations of these are very simplistic and eight are shown; the forward pair abreast the bridge should be removed. There are no indications of Carley floats anywhere.

This model forms a good basis but requires considerable enhancement to produce an accurate model.

Right: The simplistic representation of *Kent* from NT-Model.

AOSHIMA

1:700 scale

Aoshima have released kits of four different vessels – HMS *Norfolk* (3 variants), *Kent* (3 variants), *Cornwall* (2 variants) and *Dorsetshire* (3 variants including the 'Bismarck Pursuit Battle' and the 'Indian Ocean Raid'). All are very similar waterline models but have included new parts and new tooling at different times. This description is of HMS *Norfolk* (06744).

One of the first thing to notice is that the kit contains a decal of the darker areas of the camouflage pattern which greatly simplifies painting. The sheet also includes aircraft markings and a white ensign. Paint colours are specified from the CREOS range. The sprues, referred to as 'trees' in the instructions, are all shown and this diagram is worth studying as it shows that many parts on the sprues are redundant. For instance, sprue 'N' is a general sprue which is provided with numerous kits, containing aircraft, a Walrus with either folded or extended wings, plus two larger types. Sprue C2 is labelled *Dorsetshire*, and only the waterline plate is used with *Norfolk*. The hull is moulded in two halves (sprue B, again labelled *Dorsetshire*), but the superstructure parts on this sprue are unused. This approach has been used by the manufacturer to reduce the number of different sprue types required for similar vessels, in the hope of reducing costs.

The main deck is contained on sprues A1 and A2. A2 contains the forecastle with

Above: The box top artwork for HMS *Norfolk*.

wooden decking which is used rather than part 24 with a metal deck on sprue C2, which is for *Dorsetshire*. Sprue C1 contains the funnels and the superstructure sides; funnel grilles are on sprue H. Sprue F1 consists of superstructure platforms and masts; sprue F2 contains the crane.

Both sprues E and G2 are duplicated, although only the anchors and davits on sprue E are used. Each sprue E contains two primary gun turrets and sprue F three. Those on sprue F, which are of two different designs (with and without rangefinders), are specified for use. Sprue K is also duplicated and each contains nine boats (and two cabins), of which only four are used. Searchlight lenses are provided in clear plastic (sprue G1) whilst the others are grey.

This is quite a complicated kit but should produce a realistic model, which can be enhanced by the use of photoetch, and provides many 'spare' parts for other projects.

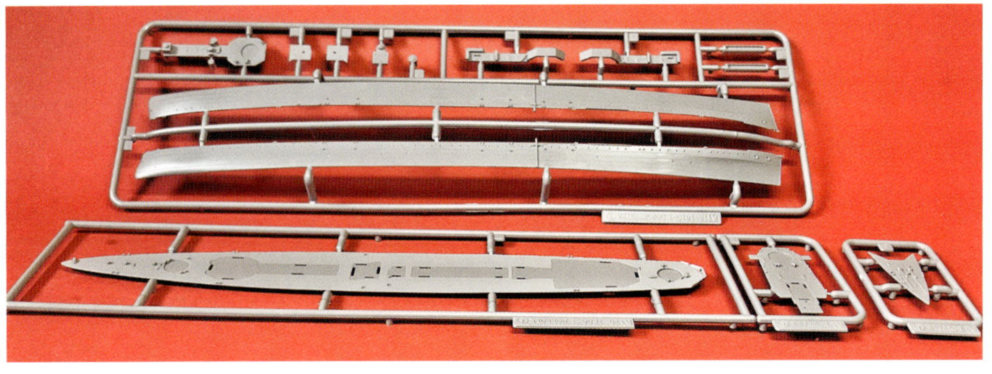

Left: The hull and deck of Aoshima's *Norfolk*.

TRUMPETER

1:700 and 1:350 scale

Trumpeter produce kits of two different vessels – HMS *Cornwall* and HMS *Kent* – at both 1:700 and 1:350 scales. The 1:700 models are waterline but the 1:350 kits contain one-piece full-hull mouldings, with stands. The most obvious difference between the two vessels is the hangar on *Cornwall*. A significant error in the kits of *Kent* is that the forecastle is moulded as wood instead of metal as carried by the vessel.

Each kit contains a full-colour sheet containing painting details; paints being specified from Mr Hobby, Acrysion, Vallejo, Model Master, Tamiya and Humbrol; showing *Cornwall* in grey and *Kent* in camouflage as worn in 1941.

Right: The two boxes for the Trumpeter 1:700 scale kits.

The 1:700 hull is a single-piece moulding with separate deck, the hulls

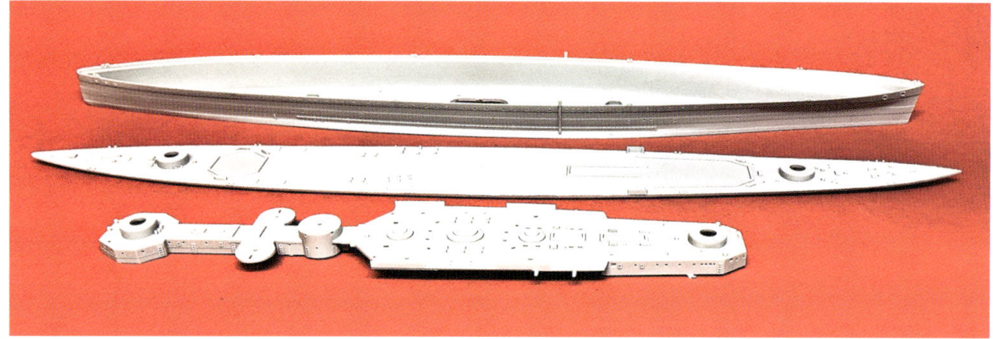

Right: The major components from Trumpeter's 1:700 scale kit of HMS *Kent*.

being identical but the decks are different. Sprues A, B and C are identical, sprue A containing the thinner funnel being duplicated, and there are four sprues B each containing a primary gun turret. Sprue C contains the central funnel. Sprue E (*Kent*) and sprue F (*Cornwall*) contains the name plate and masts. Sprues F and H (*Cornwall*) and G and J (*Kent*) contain the superstructure. Sprue MK1 is in clear plastic and contains the aircraft. Each kit contains a small photoetch sheet with crane jibs and funnel grilles. The decal sheet includes aircraft markings and flags.

The 1:350 kits also contain one-piece decks. Four sprues C contain the primary gun turrets, two sprues B the thinner funnels, with the central funnel being on sprue A. For *Cornwall*, sprues D and F provide the superstructure and sprue E the nameplate, masts and other details. Sprue MK is clear plastic and contains the aircraft. There are three photoetch sheets containing the crane gantry, funnel grilles, deck supports and railings. There is a short length of chain and the decal sheet is the same as in the smaller kits. Instructions are provided in a 16-page A4 landscape booklet.

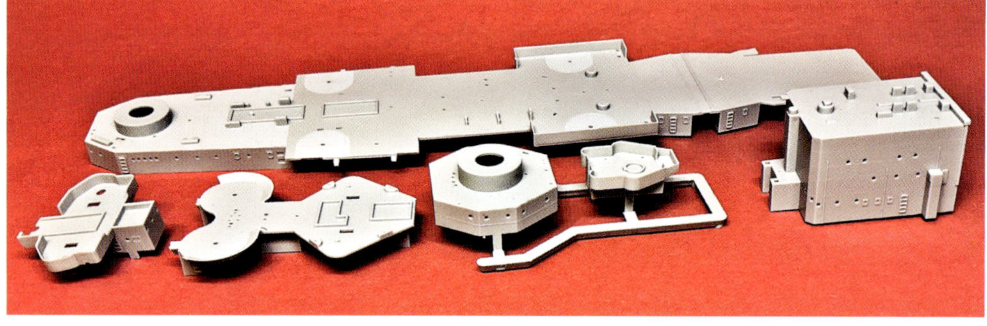

Right: The hangar and other superstructure parts from Trumpeter's 1:350 scale kit of HMS *Cornwall*.

AIRFIX 1:600 scale

Right: The full-hull and deck mouldings for HMS *Suffolk*.

The Airfix kit of HMS *Suffolk* first appeared in 1964. Since then it has been re-released at least twice, on one occasion as one of a pair with the fast minelayer HMS *Manxman*. The first box lid carried a picture of the vessel in the attractive colour scheme of the China Station (white hull and buff funnels) but when re-released (in a box of twice the volume but containing an identical kit) the box lid showed HMS *Suffolk* in an equally attractive three-colour camouflage scheme. When re-released as one of

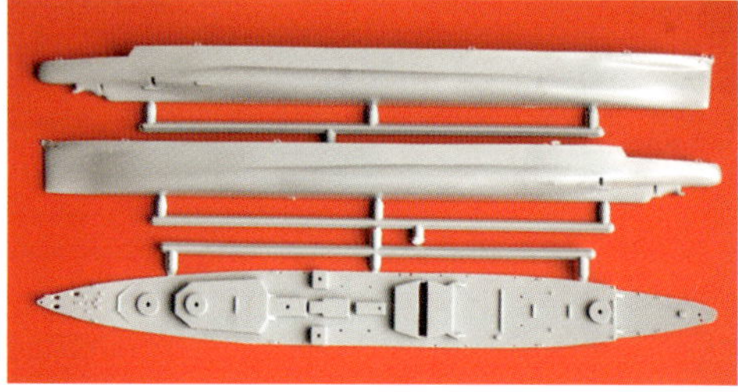

the pair, the same camouflage scheme was used. The model is moulded in light grey plastic and, as with all Airfix ship kits of this era, is a full hull model, complete with display base. Later releases of the kit do display more flash, showing some wear to the moulds.

The kit comprises the two hull halves, a full-length main deck and six sprues. The deck includes some small mouldings, such as the bollards, and the fairleads are moulded onto the hull sides. The main items of superstructure are all contained on one sprue, with one of the display supports, the other being on another sprue with the funnels, masts and cranes. Both the funnels and the cranes are each moulded in

Right: The original box (top) and the box used for the re-issue of Airfix's HMS *Suffolk*.

two halves and it is the cranes which show most noticeably the limitations of the plastic moulding techniques used. The actual framework is quite well portrayed but the mouldings are rather thick.

The main gun turrets are contained on another sprue, together with the gun barrels, the crane cabs (again in two halves) and the aircraft, the two wings being moulded separately from the fuselage. The gun barrels for the main turrets are each moulded separately but those for the AA guns are moulded in pairs. The main turrets are fixed to the deck using separate pins and so are capable of rotation when fitted.

A further sprue carries the davits and propeller shafts, another the smaller guns, boats and propellers and the final one the Carley floats and small superstructure components. The mouldings and the sprue layouts remain the same for all releases.

The instructions also remain basically the same – identical assembly diagrams but reformatted and later issues have notes in many more languages. There is a short history of the vessel's career but the colour scheme is a little confusing – light grey with buff decks and funnels, the same paint being specified for both areas of buff. Paint colours were originally specified using Airfix's own range of paints but later instructions specify paints from the Humbrol range.

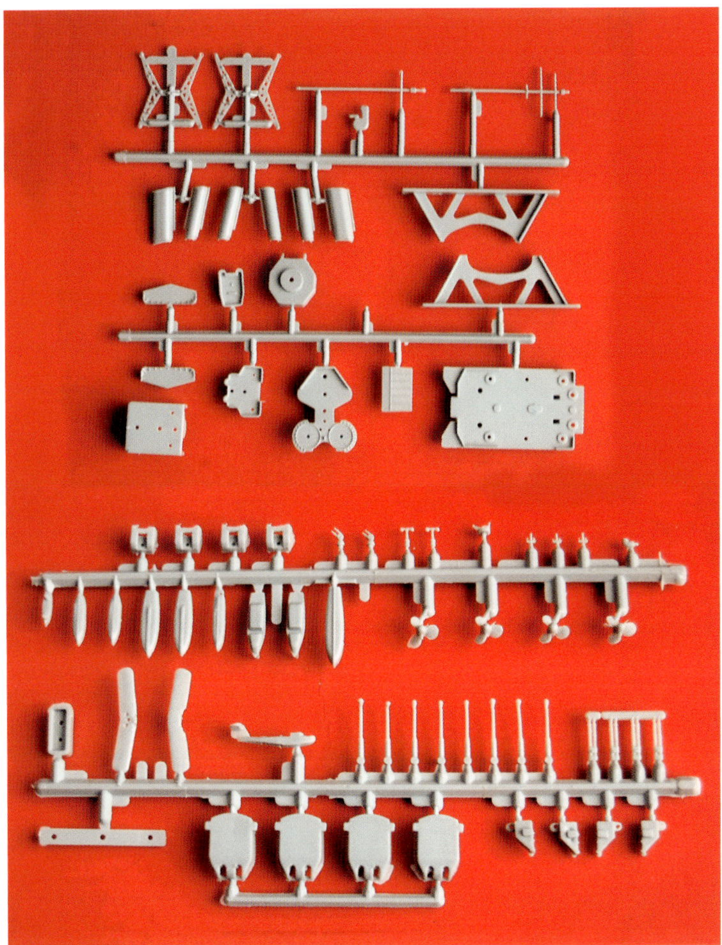

Above: The major components provided for the model of HMS *Suffolk*.

WYDAWNICTWO JSC

1:400 scale

This waterline card model of HMS *Norfolk* from Wydawnictwo JSC is contained in an A4 sized book with the model contained on four sheets of thick card, the two for the upperdeck being printed in colour whilst the two containing the basic hull structure are printed solely in black, and two sheets of thinner card, again printed solely in black. The ship's history and the instructions are in Polish but if the model is purchased from Marcle Models in the UK, a translation in English is included.

The cover includes a picture of the vessel wearing the colours of the China station and it is these colours that are used for the model. The basic hull structure on the thicker card includes the waterline in two pieces, a vertical 'keel' section and the bulkheads. The main decks are also in the thicker card with the deck planking printed on them. The thicker card is also used for the main superstructure components and some of the details. The thinner card is used for the hull sides, so that it can be bent easily to follow the hull shape, the turrets and smaller details.

The back cover, which is the same thickness as the thinner card, contains a line drawing of the ship, clearly showing the location of the components and the parts

Left: The 1:400 scale card model is contained in an A4 size book.

(printed in colour) for two Fairey IIIF biplanes. Card is not provided specifically for the gun barrels but the pattern is included, as are patterns for the masts and yards. Those who are not used to rolling card to such small diameters may prefer to use plastic rod or turned brass barrels.

FLEETSCALE/QUAYCRAFT

1:128 scale

Fleetscale (Westward Mouldings Ltd) produce a GRP hull at 1:128 scale. The hull is of HMS *Devonshire* but could equally be used to produce models of HMS *Dorsetshire* or *Sussex*. A general arrangement drawing is also included and a selection of resin accessories to complement the hull are available from Quaycraft. These accessories include the distinctive funnels and the main and secondary turrets. Other

Below: The stern of the hull moulding clearly shows the level of detail moulded into the hull.

Right: The three distinctive funnels of the 'County' class, along with two different sizes of Carley floats, as produced by Quaycraft.

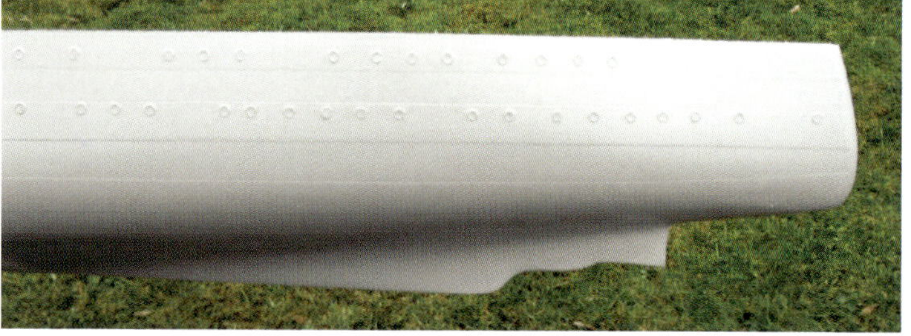

Right: The main gun turrets are supplied with separate range-finder housings and cast metal barrels.

more generic fittings, such as Carley floats, fairleads, bollards, searchlights and small calibre weapons are also available. These are cleanly and robustly moulded in lightweight resin and so are particularly suitable for working models.

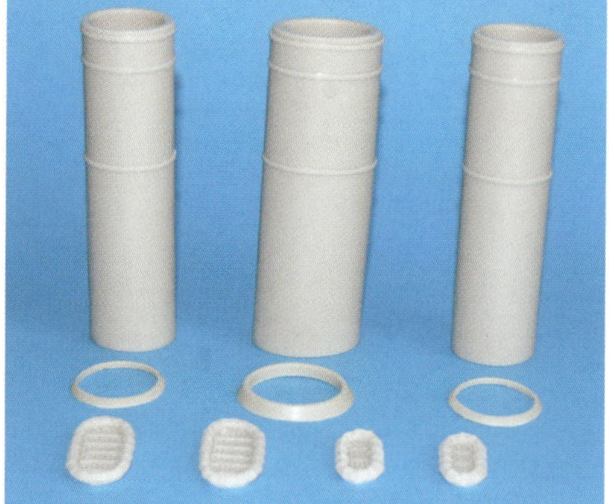

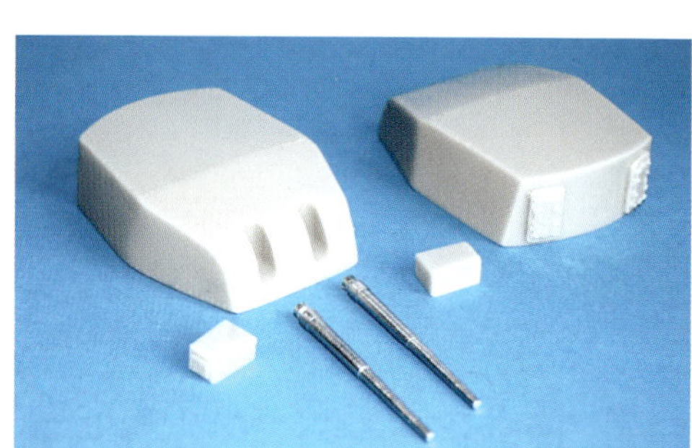

SSMODEL

1:350 scale

SSModel produce a 3D printed, full hull model of HMS *London* as in 1945. The hull is provided in six sections – above and below water; fore, midships and aft. There are nine baseplates containing the superstructure and details. Each of these has a simple protective cage around it. All parts are in dark grey apart from a few below water parts such as propellers and rudder, which are orange.

Instructions are provided on three sides of A4 consisting of diagrams showing the assembly and including diagrams of the baseplates, identifying the locations of the various parts. The three deck sections have a number of thin strands extending from the interface to details on the deck. These are to enhance the printing and are easily

Left: The three above-water hull sections.

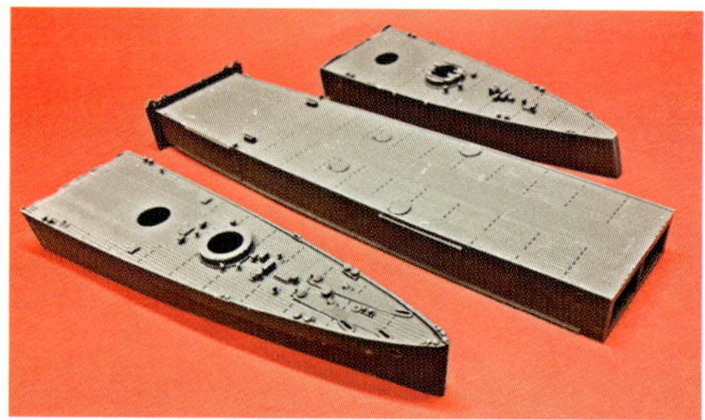

removed but there is still need for cleaning-up to remove all traces, as shown in the image. There are no location features to aid alignment although the internal structure of the interfaces do offer some possibilities. The image of a baseplate containing the major part of the superstructure has had the protective framework removed for clarity.

This kit contains a great deal of detail and can be constructed to produce a fine model. No colour details are provided so other sources must be used to complete the model.

Right: The major part of the superstructure.

Below: The front cover of HMS *Kent* by PaperModelling.

PAPERMODELLING

1:200 scale

This card model of HMS *Kent* is provided in an A3 size book containing 12 sheets of coloured card, four sheets of paper with the internal structure which will need sticking to thicker card for use, and three sides of assembly diagrams. Some of the card sheets are coloured on both sides when the part will be visible from both sides in the completed model.

This is a full-hull model with stand. The printed colours are not realistic, the camouflage in particular being very bright. The model includes a great amount of detail, which has required much research, and the colours are just limitations of the printing process – a great pity.

Accessories

WHITE ENSIGN MODELS

1:600 and 1:350 scale

White Ensign Models (UK) produced a sheet of photoetch which includes parts for the Airfix model of HMS *Suffolk*. Released in 2001, it was identified as 'WW2 British Destroyers and Escorts', although it also included parts for HMS *Suffolk* and *Manxman*.

Having moved to the USA, WEM now offer two sheets at 1:600 scale – 'Ultimate' WWII RN Destroyer/Cruiser Set 1 (PE 630) and 'Ultimate' WWII RN Destroyer/Cruiser Set 2 (PE 631). PE 630 includes parts for HMS *Campbeltown*, *Manxman*, *Cossack* and *Hotspur*, as well as *Suffolk*. Those for *Suffolk* include boat davits, 01 deck double X braces, funnel platform, large motor boat cradles, whaler cradles, 291 radar antenna, quarter deck davits, 01 deck supports, main crane jibs, crane hooks, binocular mountings, bridge windscreen, gun director yagi aerials, single X braces, bridge rangefinders, mast starfish assemblies, 279 radar antenna, mast top platform, depth charge rails, Walrus amphibian parts, cross deck catapult launch cradle, funnel cap grilles, and alternative catapult turntable and assembly.

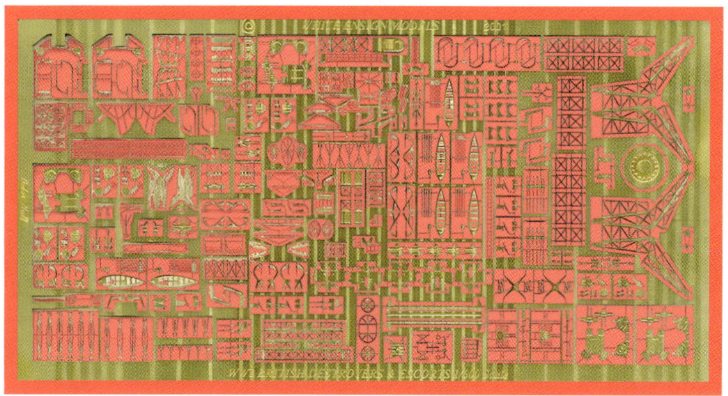

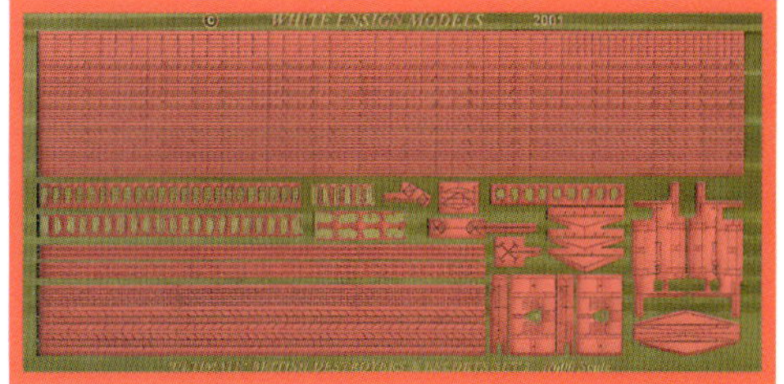

Also included on this sheet are parts for 4-barrelled pom-poms, 0.5in quad Vickers machine guns, 27ft whalers, stove pipes, and twin and single 20mm Oerlikons.

PE 631 contains the generic fittings for the same models including 2-bar railing with closer stanchions at one end, 3-bar offset railing, 3-bar standard railing, waffle pattern doors, pre-war pattern WT doors, anchor chain, ammunition locker hatches, deck hatches, DF antenna (2 types), 279 radars, 281 radars, 286 radar, 291 radar, and a selection of additional yardarm footropes.

At 1:350 scale, WEM provide PE 35188 for the Trumpeter kit of *Cornwall*. This sheet is very extensive and includes deck supports, railings, bridge details, crane details, mast details, boat davit falls, vent grilles and trunking, main director sight lens, accommodation ladders and davits, fo'c'sle breakwater, funnel siren platforms, aircraft catapult parts, depth charge rails, funnel cap grilles, radar antennas, Walrus deck handling trolley and launching cradle, 4in HA/LA gun mounting fittings, semaphore arms, ship's bell, boat fittings and cradles, small calibre gun details, Carley raft details, paravane parts, anchors, window hatches, inclined and vertical ladders, 8in gun turret access doors, various hatches, cable and cordage reels, watertight doors and anchor chain.

Above: WEM's PE 631.

Left: WEM's PE 630.

Below: WEM's PE 35188.

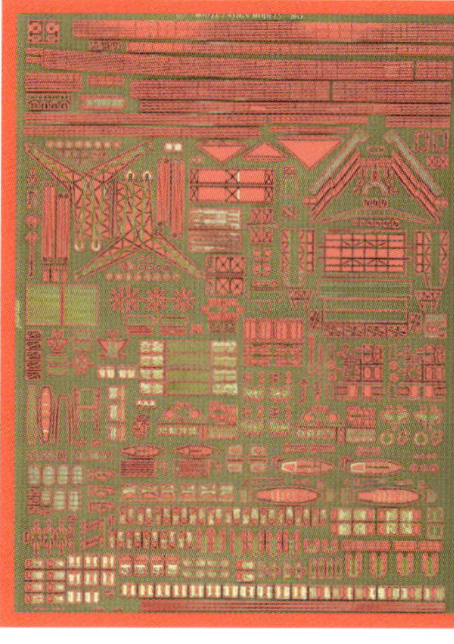

ATLANTIC MODELS

1:600 scale

Following the closure of WEM in the UK, Peter Hall of Atlantic Models, who had designed the photoetch for WEM, released some enhanced sheets of photoetch for individual vessels, including ATEM 60015 HMS *Suffolk* Detail Set.

Included are railings, WT doors, funnel sirens and platforms, bulwarks, deck supports, hangar doors, pom-pom and 4in gun shields, aircraft crane details, Walrus details, catapult details, depth charge rails, radar antennae, boat details, cable reels, accommodation ladder and davits, mast top sensor, funnel cap grilles, anchors, small calibre gun details, mast details, breakwater, 8in gun turret doors, ladders, anchor chain, ensign and jack staffs, and deck hatches.

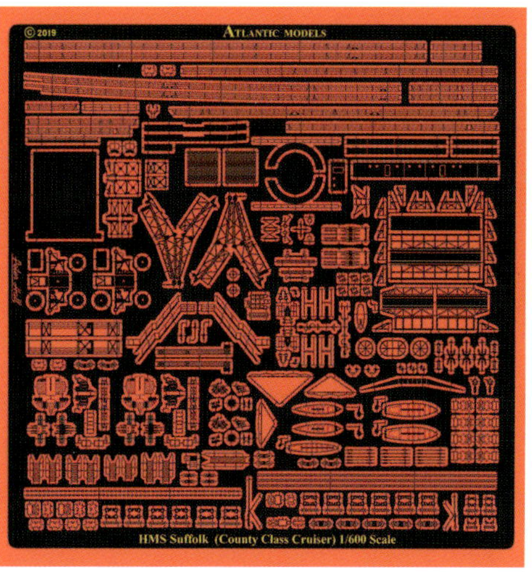

Left: Atlantic Models ATEM 60015

TOM'S MODELWORKS

1:700 scale

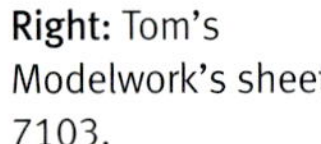
Right: Tom's Modelwork's sheet 7103.

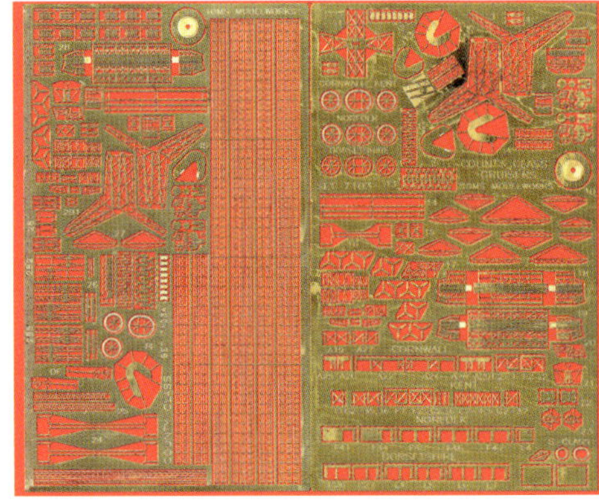

Sheet 7103 is designed for the Aoshima 'County' class kits of *Dorsetshire*, *Norfolk*, *Cornwall*, and *Kent*. Any two kits can be detailed using this set, which includes railings, cranes, catapults, radar antennas and many other parts specific to each kit. Many of these Aoshima kits come with bonus or extra aircraft and there are parts to detail Walrus amphibians, Wellington bombers, Sunderland flying boats, SM.79 torpedo bombers, and even an old 'S' class destroyer.

SHIPYARD WORKS

1:350 scale

This Chinese company produces a detail set S350006 for use with the Trumpeter model of *Kent* (05352). It includes twelve sheets of photoetch, some turned brass items including masts and gun barrels, and some 3D printed items. These items are not mentioned on the

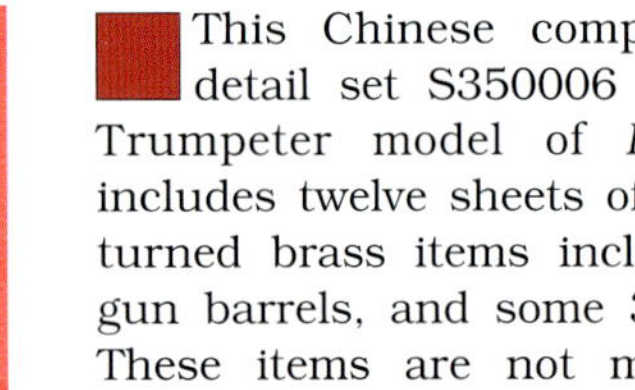

instruction sheet as they are additions to the original release and duplicate some parts which can be made from the photoetch sheets, *eg* the octuple pom-pom mounts. This will certainly simplify the use of this set.

There is also a self-adhesive wooden deck. Parts provided include crane details, aircraft and catapult details, boat details, mast and funnel details, radar antennas, as well as additional platforms, watertight doors and other deck details. The twin 4in guns are provided on the photoetch sheets, but these are very complex assemblies. There is a large double-sided sheet of instructions which require careful study if optimum use is to be made of this comprehensive set.

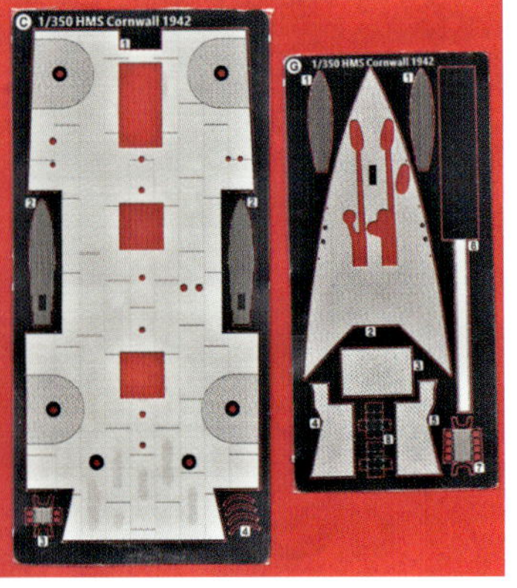

Above: The 3D printed parts are produced in a black material.

Right: The self-adhesive wooden deck is provided in seven main sections, with details for the boats.

VERY FIRE TECHNOLOGY

1:350 scale

Right: The primary and secondary gun mountings.

Below: The two photo-etch deck sections.

This Chinese company produces a detail set VF350024 for use with the Trumpeter model of *Cornwall* (05353). It includes eight sheets of photoetch, some turned brass items including masts, gun barrels and bollards, and some resin parts, including primary and secondary gun mountings, the latter comprising three components, searchlights, Carley floats (two different sizes), winches, capstans and paravanes. There is also a self-adhesive wooden deck and a short length of anchor chain.

The photoetch includes two deck sections (forecastle and amidships), a complete set of guardwires, and details for

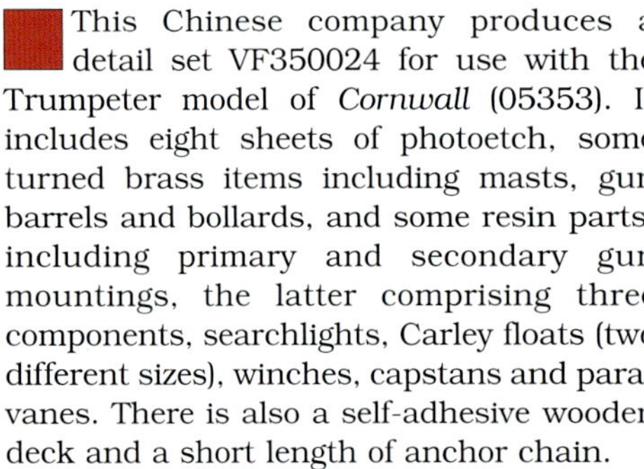

the crane, boats and aircraft, as well as watertight doors and other superstructure details. Once again, the very extensive instruction sheets require careful study to make optimum use of this set.

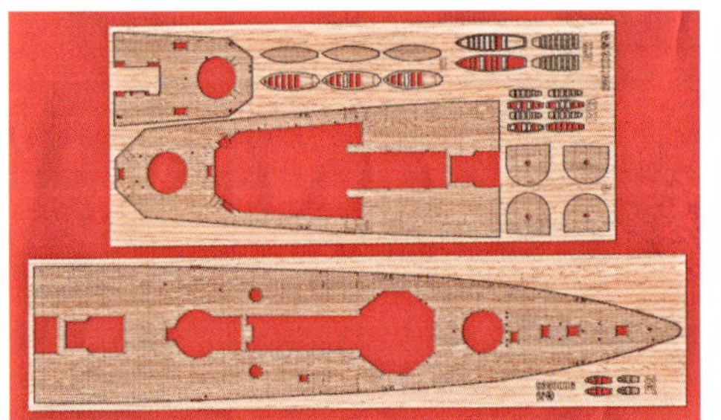

MICRO MASTER

1:700, 1:600 and 1:350 scale

Right: The two sets of funnels, high and low platforms, at 1:350 scale.

This New Zealand company produces a wide range of 3D printed warship accessories for a number of different navies at a variety of scales, including 1:700, 1:600 and 1:350. The range of items produced for the Royal Navy includes gun mountings, varying in calibre from 0.5in to 16in, torpedo tubes, depth charges and rails and throwers, boats from 10ft to 50ft long, Carley floats, searchlights, fire control directors, doors and hatches, lockers, vents and anchors.

SWORDFISH MODELS

1:350 scale

The Belgian company of Swordfish Models produces a wide range of 'Royal Navy WW2' accessories at 1:350 scale. These include gun mountings up to 5.25in calibre, gun directors, bridge and deck equipment, torpedo tubes, depth charges and boats. They also produce accessories for the American, German, Japanese, Italian and French navies, as well as smaller ranges of accessories at the larger scales of 1:200, 1:144 and 1:72.

Of particular interest is the director control tower for the 'County' class cruisers, which is available with or without the Type 284 radar at 1:350 scale. All the products are sold in stiff plastic boxes to protect the fine detail.

Swordfish Models subsequently (late 2025) released an upgrade set for the Trumpeter *Kent* which contains: 4 x 8in twin turrets (two with 2 x 20mm Oerlikons

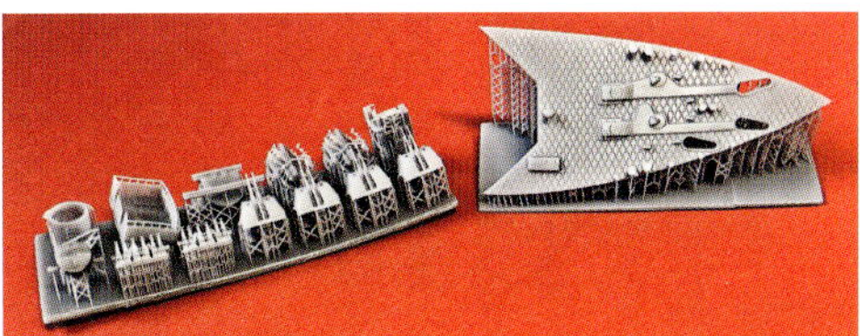

and ammunitions boxes on top); 4 x 4in mountings; 2 x octuple 2pdr mountings; 2 x quad 0.5in Vickers mountings; 2 x 20mm Oerlikon guns; directors; foredeck; capstans; open bridge and bridge equipment; searchlights; cable reels; vents; winches; deck and ammunition lockers; hatches, doors and scuttles; boats with cradles; cranes; aircraft catapult; Carley floats; complete rear structure with 2pdr platforms and searchlight tower; and 3 funnels.

The three A4 instruction sheets are provided in pdf format by e-mail. They identify all the components by number, contain colour illustrations identifying the location of the larger parts and a deck plan identifying their locations by part number. The inclusion of these highly detailed and finely printed components will enhance any model, as well as correcting kit errors – highly recommended.

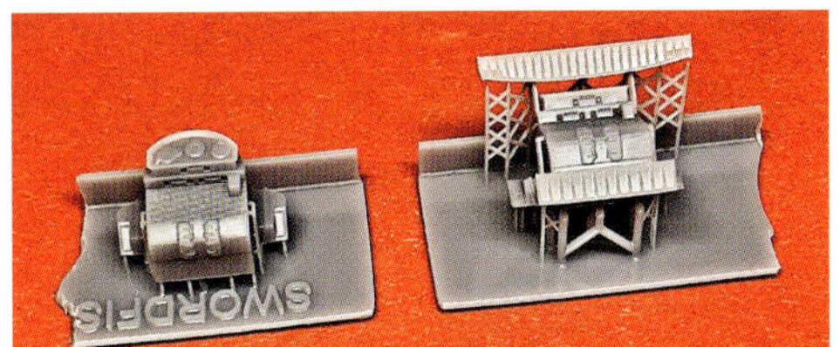

Right: The replacement 'metal' forecastle and AA weapons.

Right: The two gunfire control directors, with and without radar Type 284.

KRAKEN HOBBIES

1:350 scale

This 3D printed set is to convert the Trumpeter kit of *Kent* to the ill-fated cruiser *Canberra*. The set includes the Oerlikon 20mm tubs on top of the primary turrets, 01 deck, signal and open bridges, forward and main battery directors, Type 271 radar array, Type A290 air search radar, 2 x 20mm Oerlikon bandstands, 3 x funnels (including the additional 3 feet added to the RAN cruisers), forward engine room vent deckhouse, deckhouse below the second funnel, AA gun deck with integrated deckhouses and catapult tower, including walkway from 01 deck, 3 x petrol storage tanks, 2 x 21in quadruple torpedo tubes, aft deck structure, aft control and searchlight director platform, auxiliary main battery director, searchlight platform with offset tub and mount for HACS, aft 20mm gun tub, 4 x 4in twin AA guns, 12 x 20mm Oerlikons.

This set also includes an extensive set of instructions, 19 A4 sides, detailing the loca-

tion of each part and their integration with the Trumpeter kit. The instructions also include a short history of the cruiser and colour details – an Admiralty camouflage pattern in early 1942 and 'Chicago Blue' later in the year when operating with the USN. This is a very detailed, and interesting, conversion set – highly recommended for more adventurous modellers.

Right: Two of the replacement super-structures and the three heightened funnels.

CHUANYU MODEL SHIP

1:350 scale

This Chinese company produces a self-adhesive wooden deck for the Trumpeter *Kent*. This comprises three main deck areas and five smaller platforms, replicating the error of the kit by including a wooden forecastle. This should be removed before use. The deck is supplied with brass barrels for both the primary and secondary armament, and a length of anchor chain.

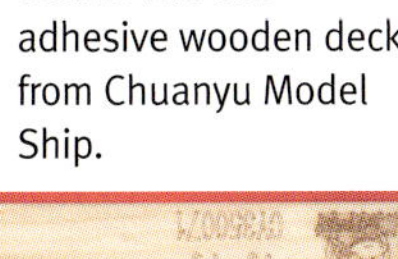

Below: The self-adhesive wooden deck from Chuanyu Model Ship.

Modelmakers' Showcase

HP MODELS **HMS *LONDON*** 1:700 scale   By ANTHONY CHU

This model was the result of close co-operation between two modellers – Anthony Chu who built the model and Dimi Apostolopoulos who carried out the research, now owns the model and supplied the photographs.

A number of modifications were needed in order to depict the cruiser as in late summer of 1942. A large number of photographs were used as reference to detail the model. For example, the photographs showed that the decks were painted in a dark grey. They also showed a great deal of detail on the construction of the bridge and armament.

HMS *BERWICK* (BASED ON TRUMPETER HMS *CORNWALL*) 1:350 scale

By ROB MATTHEWS

This was built to portray HMS *Berwick* as she appeared in 1940. The base kit used was the Trumpeter HMS *Cornwall* 1:350 offering. An adhesive wooden deck was used together with numerous Micromaster 3D pieces including the ship's boats and anti-aircraft armament. White Ensign Models PE sets were also used extensively and rigging was completed using Infini lycra thread. The base was Styrofoam painted, then textured with Liquitex gloss medium and finally finished with several layers of Liquitex high gloss varnish.

TRUMPETER **HMS *KENT*** 1:350 scale
By ROB MATTHEWS

This was built from the Trumpeter 1:350 kit. Assembly was straightforward with the exception of the forecastle deck which is wrongly moulded as wood in the kit. I replaced this with a piece of etched metal to represent the actual steel deck that *Kent* sported. Extensive use was made of the excellent Micromaster 3D print offerings including the 8in gun turrets, all of the secondary anti-aircraft armament, ship's boats and HACs. A limited amount of photo-etch is supplied with the kit but further detailing and ship's railings came from White Ensign Model PE sets. The colour scheme suggested in the instructions is most likely wrong and the scheme represented in my build was arrived at with the expert help of Richard Dennis and Jamie Duff. All the available evidence suggests this is the paint scheme *Kent* would have worn in 1941. Sovereign Colourcoats paints were used throughout.

COMBRIG **HMS _BERWICK_** 1:700 scale

By MIKE McCABE

Mike has portrayed his model of HMS _Berwick_ in the China Station colours as worn when on Far East service in the late 1920s and 1930s. It is built from the Combrig _Canberra_ kit, which is a good, accurate and sharply cast model but a little light on detail for such a large ship. To add detail he used a combination of photo-etch for doors, railings, crane and aircraft catapult. A large number of vents were built from plastic rod, the rear superstructure was rebuilt and brass barrels and masts replaced the resin parts in the kit. Small weapons are by Niko and finally the aircraft, a Fairey Flycatcher, was scratch-built with plastic rod, card and paper with etched brass details.

SCRATCH-BUILT **HMS *BERWICK*** 1:350 scale

By PHIL REEDER

This scratch-built model of HMS *Berwick* represents the cruiser as she appeared in 1945. Phil was commissioned to build this model for a former member of the crew who was serving on her at that time. Most of the model was built using plasticard with many items from Phil's spares locker. The turrets and funnels came from a now dismantled Iron Shipwright kit of the *Norfolk*. Whilst researching the model, Phil came to the conclusion that no two 'Counties' were the same; they all varied a great deal. He used the Profile Morskie book on the *Kent* as a guide and the Man O'War book on the 'Counties' as his main references.

COMBRIG **HMAS _AUSTRALIA_** 1:700 scale

By MIN HIN CHONG

The model was built from the Combrig resin kit. It was a fairly straightforward build but a lot of additional detail (see below) was added. The model depicts *Australia* as she appeared in 1941. Min could not find drawings of her in this time period, so photographic references were used extensively.

The following modifications were made to the kit:

- 20mm gun tubs on turrets, fantail and bridge wings deleted
- Resin anchors replaced with photo-etch anchors from Tom's Modelworks
- Moulded-on anchor chains removed and replaced with miniature chain
- Doorway cut into breakwater
- Periscopes added to main gun turret cheeks from strip styrene
- Main gun barrels replaced with turned metal items from Clipper Models
- Deck vents, scratch-built from styrene rod, added to main deck
- Photo-etch doors, ladders and hatches added to the superstructure
- Bridge wing supports scratch-built from styrene and photo-etch from White Ensign Models
- Details, such as binoculars and

compass, added to open bridge from the spares box
– Splinter mattresses scratch-built from styrene and added to upper bridge level area behind the main mast and director tower
– Masts constructed from brass wire
– Type 286 radar added to mainmast from Tom's Modelworks photo-etch set
– Scratch-built searchlight platforms adjacent to fore funnel, searchlights coming from the spares box
– Ammo boxes from the spares box added to main deck
– Additional pair of ship's boat's added from spares box
– Photo-etch boat chocks and oars from White Ensign Models added to boats
– Splinter shields around 4in AA mounts scratch-built from styrene
– Vision slit covers added to 4in AA shields
– Whistle platform added to fore funnel from White Ensign Models
– Funnel piping replaced with styrene rod
– Funnel cap grills modified from White Ensign Models photo-etch
– Cranes scratch-built from styrene tube, resin and photo-etch from White Ensign Models
– Torpedo tube housing scratch-built from styrene
– Aircraft catapult from White Ensign Models photo-etch
– Walrus aircraft from Trumpeter with White Ensign Models photo-etch added
– Pom-poms replaced with resin and photo-etch from White Ensign Models
– Aft searchlight platforms constructed from White Ensign Models photo-etch, the searchlight coming from the spares box
– Boat davits from Hasegawa photo-etch
– Photo-etch railing from White Ensign Models
– Ship and aircraft rigged with paintbrush bristles for heavy cable and Uni-Caenis fly-tying line for finer lines

WHITE ENSIGN MODELS HMS *SUSSEX* 1:700 scale By PETER FULGONEY

Peter had bought this kit from White Ensign Models in 2004 as it was in their rare sale event at a reasonable price together with three other kits. He did start this one first but about halfway through thought it might be a good idea to save the progress, and try out lesser kits so as not to make a mess of what looked to be a very good build exercise.

Peter picked up the work again in 2006 after having viewed a Royal Navy recruiting film featuring HMS *London*, another 'County' class cruiser but very unlike HMS *Sussex*, having been completely rebuilt. What he saw that could be reproduced was the retrieval of the Supermarine Walrus spotter aircraft. When the aircraft was

coming into land, the ship would make a turn at about 6 knots which creates a calm flat sea to one side. In a rougher sea this is very useful and helps reduce accidents for the seaplane crew and machine.

By 2006, and after a couple of years more experience in modelling, Peter believed he could do the kit justice. What he liked about White Ensign Models was the thoroughness of the presentation, which included very fine detailed resin, dedicated photo-etch, and fully explained instructions with a colour picture of the ship showing accurate Royal Navy painting schemes cross-referenced with their own range of paints called Colourcoats. If you like the ship rigged, then the illustration covers this but you will have to provide your own thread of choice. White Ensign Models have their own type of lycra, stretchy thread which Peter found difficult

to use in as much as it frays at the end and needs some fine attention to achieve a satisfactory result. Also the thread is white so again needs attention unless your happy with this. Peter has used stretched sprue on this kit but now use Caenis 20-denier thread together with stationery gum to fix it in place.

Everything the modeller requires, therefore, is in the package or within easy reach, saving having to trawl through references to verify information and check suspect detail on the ship. The net result was therefore a straightforward build subject and Peter feels that the model is excellent on many levels.

WHITE ENSIGN MODELS **HMS *SUSSEX*** 1:700 scale　　By RICHARD PRICE

Compared to other (more recent) releases from White Ensign Models, Richard feels that this kit was merely 'OK'. In his opinion, this lack of quality was down to the casting process; although the resin was relatively bubble free, many of the superstructure parts were out of shape and in need of work, and the hull dipped toward the stern where photos and drawings indicate a gentle upward curve. Despite this, the fine detail was very good in places, the deck planking being particularly of note.

The hull was also very bland in appearance, requiring that the scuttles (portholes) be re-drilled as they were virtually non-existent. In addition, a brass strip was inserted along the line of the bow knuckle for sharp definition, fore and aft plating was simulated by fixing paper strip saturated in superglue, some scuttles were plated over using PE discs and open scuttles were given rigols (eyebrows) using fine wire salvaged from a small electric motor.

Richard chose to cut the superstructure parts into discrete blocks, completely removing them from the decks. This allowed him to square up the deck housings and sharpen up corners, and replace overhanging decks with thin brass sheet. It also meant that a lot of the deck fittings were remade from scratch or from PE and detail sets bought separately. The area receiving the most reworking was probably the bridge. The original castings had very thick splinter-shielding which was nowhere near tall enough. The original castings were split into each level, removing all decks in the process, new decks being completely scratch-built from 2 and 5 thou brass sheet with new splinter shields, blast bags (photo references show these) and wind deflectors.

The bridge supports are from the original PE set.

Weaponry was a mixed bag. The main turrets were modified to clean up the casting and to reshape the front, which looks more rounded in photos compared to the rather angular cast items, and given brass barrels. The secondary HA armament included was pretty good but Richard wanted to try the Flyhawk versions which were amazing, though considerably more stressful to assemble. He also used the Flyhawk pom-poms over the WEM ones as they have solid ammunition containers with some nice etched detail. 20mms were from the included PE set. Torpedo tubes were scratch-built – to an excessive extent, with real tube construction and little torpedo heads added (for painting purposes), none of which can be seen on the finished model! Richard now thinks that they should have been fixed with one of the mounts pointing outboard.

Gun directors were a mix of scratch-built structures with either WEM or Flyhawk antenna. Richard admits he loves the Flyhawk PE stuff but it is somewhat for the masochists. Ships boats were completely replaced. Where available

Richard used resin parts from Admiralty Models, but they did not do a large pinnace, so more scratch-building was required: a very time-consuming effort but worth it as these have real visible depth of interior.

Painting was done using WEM Colourcoats throughout (a great product which pretty much allows 'painting-by-numbers') and weathered using various washes and filters.

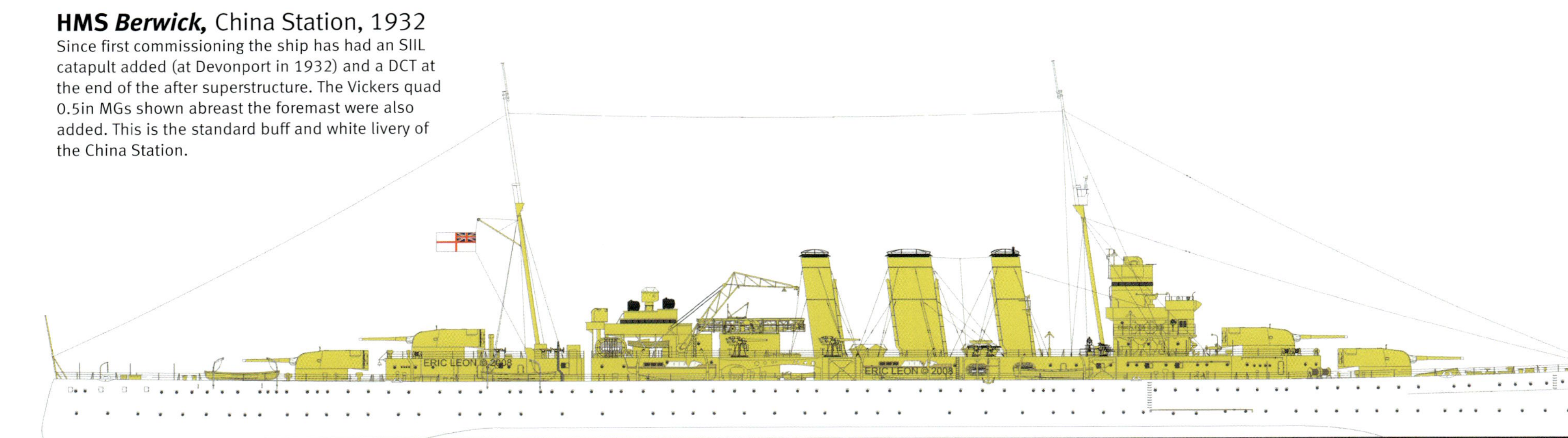

HMS *Berwick*, China Station, 1932

Since first commissioning the ship has had an SIIL catapult added (at Devonport in 1932) and a DCT at the end of the after superstructure. The Vickers quad 0.5in MGs shown abreast the foremast were also added. This is the standard buff and white livery of the China Station.

HMS *Suffolk*, April 1940

The first pair to undergo a major modernisation in the mid-1930s, *Cumberland* and *Suffolk*, both had their quarterdecks cut down because of fears that their displacement might exceed treaty limits. This is a reconstruction of the camouflage scheme worn during the Norway campaign (507B and 507C), when the ship was heavily damaged; the starboard side pattern is known to have been different, but there is insufficient data for an illustration.

HMS *Berwick,* November 1940

After a major reconstruction between July 1937 and November 1938, the ship emerged with a hangar and fixed cross-deck catapult, a remodelled bridge surmounted by a new DCT and HA directors each side. The AA armament was upgraded to four twin 4in Mk XIX mountings and two 8-barrelled 2pdr pom-poms (abreast the forward funnels).

This scheme, comprising dark (507B) and light (507C) grey, was worn by the ship when deployed to the Mediterranean in November 1940 and represents her appearance at the Battle of Cape Spartivento. The decks were unpainted wood and the turret tops 507C. This was the same scheme carried during the Norway campaign earlier in the year except that the hull was then dark grey (507B).

All illustrations © Eric Leon

HMS *Kent,* September 1940

Heavier than her sisters when completed, *Kent* was not given a hangar in her major pre-war refit, but she did receive a heavy EIVH catapult capable of launching a Walrus amphibian. This configuration is essentially her appearance as she entered the war, with no additions to her AA armament – the existing light AA is concentrated around the lattice searchlight tower aft, with the 2pdr pom-poms on the shelter deck and the quad 0.5in MGs on a platform above and abaft of them. Note that in the camouflage pattern the dark and light greys are separated by a thin strip of medium grey.

HMS *Berwick,* February 1942

During a refit at Rosyth the ship had five single 20mm added (on the tops of B and X turrets, right aft on the quarterdeck, and two on the hangar roof). The ship is painted in 507A and 507C, with white to represent a false bow wave and wake; decks and turret tops were dark grey.

HMAS *Canberra*, May 1942

The Australian 'Counties' received less modification than their RN sisters and after her last wartime refit in 1942 HMAS *Canberra* – as shown here – still had single 4in HA guns and no 2pdr pom-poms, although at least six 20mm Oerlikons were added. She was also fitted with Type 271 radar on top of the fire control tower. This camouflage scheme of 507A, 507C with patches of white was supposedly replaced with an overall coat of US Navy 'Chicago blue' before the ship's loss at Guadalcanal in August 1942.

All illustrations © Eric Leon

HMS *Suffolk,* June 1942

This basic pattern was carried from the spring of 1941 – including during the *Bismarck* action – although the white was not added to the tops of the funnels and hangar until June 1942. The colours were 507A, MS3 and 507C.

HMS *Berwick,* December 1943

In the summer of 1942 the ship had the aircraft arrangements removed and replaced by a new superstructure topped by a Type 273 radar lantern. After a further refit in August – December 1943 at Rosyth the ship emerged in this configuration. AA enhancements included seven twin 20mm mountings (one right aft, and the rest on the shelter deck – two between the third funnel and the after superstructure and one abreast the foremast, port and starboard).

The colour shades of this scheme are not known for certain, but may be 507C, B55, G10 and B30; the decks were dark grey and turret tops dark or medium grey. The 4in gun shields also appear to be darker than any other colours.

All illustrations © Eric Leon

HMS *Berwick*, May 1945

This is the standard late-war two-tone scheme (B20 and G45) with the addition of some white in the upperworks.

HMS *Sussex*, April 1945

In her last wartime refit early in 1945 *Sussex* had X turret removed and both light AA and electronics considerably enhanced. The ship now mounts six 8-barrelled 2pdr pom-poms, four twin and four single 20mm Oerlikons. The ship wears the standard late-war two-tone scheme (B20 and G45).

All illustrations © Eric Leon

Continued from p.16

HMAS *AUSTRALIA*

Modifications. As was also true of *Canberra*, modifications to *Australia* pre-war were very limited. *Australia* received her catapult in 1935. However, she was refitted along broadly similar lines to *Kent* between April 1938 and August 1939, although her replacement twin 4in guns were positioned on the main deck and not the boat deck. By 1943 she also carried seven 20mm Oerlikons. These were replaced by seven twins early in 1944, and seven single 40mm Bofors were added by 1945.

Wartime highlights. During the first four months of the war, *Australia* was deployed in her home waters and in June 1940 she operated off Norway and was in the Atlantic at the beginning of July, before being diverted to support operations against the Vichy French at Dakar, West Africa, where she operated with the aircraft carrier *Hermes*. At the end of the month *Australia* sailed with the battlecruisers *Repulse* and *Renown*, and the cruisers *Sheffield*, *York* and her sister *Devonshire* in an unsuccessful search for the German battleship *Gneisenau*. August was spent in a search for blockade runners off Bear Island and at the beginning of September she was involved in the support of Vichy French landings at Dakar (Operation Menace).

Having been the target of an unsuccessful torpedo attack by *U36*, *Australia* relieved her sister *Cumberland* on interception patrol off Dakar in the middle of the month and was involved in the interception of some French cruisers that were attempting to break out of Dakar, escorting *Gloire* and *Montcalm* to Casablanca. On 23 September *Australia* was involved in an engagement with three Vichy French destroyers attempting to leave Dakar, during which the flotilla leader *L'Audacieux* was damaged by 8in gunfire and set on fire. She then took part in the initial bombardment of Dakar, during which her Walrus aircraft was shot down whilst carrying out spotting duties and she sustained two hits from shore fire with little damage.

At the beginning of October *Australia* covered the Free French landings at Douala and returned to RAN control in November 1941. In mid-February 1942 *Australia* joined the ANZAC Squadron on its formation and was deployed in the SW Pacific under overall US Navy command. Following a period in the Coral Sea, the ANZAC Squadron was disbanded at the end of March but the Australian ships remained under US Navy command for convoy defence duties. At the beginning of May *Australia* was deployed as part of TF44 in support of TF17 during US operations against the Japanese invasion of New Guinea (Battle of the Coral Sea), coming under air attacks but incurring no damage.

After taking part in convoy defence duties in the SW Pacific, *Australia* joined her sister *Canberra* as part of TG62.1 at the end of July, the two Australian ships providing cover for the US landings on Tulagi at the beginning of August. At the end of the month she joined TF44, along with the Australian cruiser *Hobart*, during the support of operations against the Japanese invasion in New Guinea. *Australia*

Below left: The bridge of *Australia* as built, with the tall fire control tower surmounted by a small rangefinder-director. The windows were designed to give all-round visibility to the spotting team within. Note also the rangefinders on pedestals in the bridge wings.

Below right: In a telling contrast to the ship as built, *Australia*'s bridge in 1948 sports an elaborate suite of late-war British radars.

A good broadside view of *Australia* on 31 August 1942 taken from the US carrier *Wasp* (CV-7). The ship still carries an aircraft and catapult, but the main topmast has been struck and there are 20mm gun positions ahead of, and on the roof of, B turret, and on X turret and the extreme stern.

The open bridge of *Australia* in September 1944. Most of these personnel, including the captain, were to be killed the following month when the ship was crashed by a Japanese bomber.

remained with TF44 until being transferred to the US 7th Fleet in February 1943 when she became part of TF74, initially forming part of TG74.3.

From March to May, *Australia* continued as part of TF74, and towards the end of June, the task force covered US amphibious operation in New Georgia (Operation Cartwheel) and in mid-July, was diverted to reinforce US ships supporting the landings in New Georgia. In November *Australia* was sent to reinforce South Pacific forces and, in December, covered landing by the VII Amphibious Force in Arawe, New Britain (Operation Director). On Boxing Day she provided naval gunfire support for the landing of the 1st US Marine Division at Cape Gloucester, New Guinea and at the beginning of 1944 provided cover for the landing of the 32nd US Infantry Division near Saidor, New Guinea (Operation Dexterity).

Having undergone a refit in February and March, *Australia* rejoined TF74 in April and covered landings of the 1st US Corps in New Guinea at Hollandia (Operation Reckless) and Aitape (Operation Persecution). It was the turn of 41st US Infantry Division to receive cover at the end of May on the south coast of Biak Island (Operation Horlicks). In the middle of July, she bombarded Japanese troops at Aitape and in September transferred to TF75 along with other RAN ships. In the middle of the month she provided naval gunfire support for the landings of US troops on Morotai and in the middle of the following month supported preparatory operations for the assault on the Philippines. On 21 October a Japanese bomber crashed into *Australia*'s bridge structure during the Battle of Leyte Gulf causing serious damage with many casualties. She returned to the British Fleet base at Manus for repairs, rejoining the US 7th Fleet at the end of November.

In January 1945 *Australia* was deployed with her sister *Shropshire* as part of TG77.2 for support of the Luzon landings. On the 6th when entering Lingayen Gulf to provide naval gunfire support she was hit by a Kamikaze aircraft and sustained major damage. Two days later she was hit by four more Kamikaze aircraft and sustained further damage and many casualties. The next day she once again came under Kamikaze attacks, being hit again, and so withdrew from operations and took passage to Leyte for temporary repairs and then on to Australia for permanent repairs, which lasted until August.

Australia was re-commissioned after her repairs and rejoined the Australian Fleet. She remained in commission until August 1954 when she paid-off and was placed on the disposal list, being sold in January 1955 for demolition.

HMAS *CANBERRA*

Modifications. Apart from the installation of aircraft facilities and the addition of 0.5in machine guns, *Canberra* received little pre-war modification. In 1942, when she was under refit, her close range AA defence was improved by the fitting of at least six 20mm Oerlikon guns, but the planned pair of multiple 2pdr pom-pom

were never mounted, nor did she receive four extra 4in guns.

Wartime highlights. At the beginning of World War II *Canberra* was deployed in the Indian Ocean, transferring to RN control in May 1940. After a refit in January 1941 she intercepted the German freighter *Coburg*, which was accompanied by the captured Norwegian tanker *Ketty Brovig*, at the beginning of March. In May she transferred to the newly formed ANZAC Squadron and at the end of January 1942 she transferred for service under overall US Navy command. On May 30 *Canberra* was at Sydney during the Japanese midget submarine attacks on shipping and on 10 July sailed from Sydney, with her sister *Australia*, to form part of TF44 for the support of US amphibious operations in the SW Pacific. On the night of 9 August *Canberra* was in action with the Japanese cruisers *Chokai*, *Aoba*, *Kako*, *Kinugasa* and *Furutaka* south of Savo Island. She was set on fire and received major damage after repeated hits by gunfire and by four torpedoes; 84 of ship's company were killed and she had to be abandoned the following morning, the wreck being sunk by a US destroyer.

HMS *DEVONSHIRE*

Modifications. World War II intervened during the reconstruction of *London* and so the similar rebuilds planned for *Devonshire*, *Sussex* and *Shropshire* did not take place. However, they did receive their aircraft facilities and in 1936-37 their AA armament was enhanced by the installation of four further 4in single mountings and two quad 0.5in MGs. In 1941 two multiple 2pdr pom-poms and four single 20mm were added, and tripods strengthened the masts to enable the aircraft warning radar Type 281 to be carried; Type 285 fire control radar was also fitted. In February 1942 a surface warning radar Type 273 was fitted between B turret and the bridge. *Devonshire* later replaced the eight singles with four twin 4in mountings fitted and her close range AA armament was increased by four more 20mm. By the end of 1943 two quad 2pdrs were added, and twelve twin 20mm replaced all but two of the single Oerlikons.

During May 1943 to March 1944, *Devonshire* underwent a refit which included the removal of X turret and the catapult; radar Type 281 was replaced by Type 281B which required the use of only one mast for siting

Above: One of the last photos of *Canberra*, taken on 22 July 1942. The ship has been fitted with Type 271 radar abaft the 8in director, and there are pairs of single 20mm Oerlikons on B and X turret, and replacing the 0.5in MGs on the shelter deck abaft the bridge.

Below: A US Navy photo of *Devonshire*, dated 21 March 1942 but possibly taken earlier as there is no Type 273 lantern forward of the bridge (fitted in February 1942). The ship still has single 4in guns, but there is an octuple 2pdr pom-pom abreast the after superstructure. The camouflage is two shades of grey, 507A and 507C, and the pattern is mirror-imaged on the port side.

Devonshire on 29 June 1944 after her major refit of 1943/44, with X turret and catapult removed and the Type 273 lantern relocated amidships.

the aerial. Additional fire control radar outfits were added and the surface warning radar Type 273 was repositioned amidships. IFF equipment was added to the radar outfit. At this point the ship's light AA comprised six quad 2pdrs, seven twin 20mm and four single 20mm. In 1945 additional 20mm gun mountings were added, making seventeen twins and six singles in total.

After the war, *Devonshire* was taken in hand for conversion to a Cadet Training Ship by HM Dockyard, Devonport in September 1946. Her main armament, except A turret, was removed along with some AA weapons, and extensive changes were made to provide accommodation and instructional facilities.

Wartime highlights. *Devonshire* was in the Mediterranean with the 1st Cruiser Squadron at the declaration of war and underwent some repairs to her rudder at Malta in October, returning to Alexandria on completion of the repairs. At the beginning of November she sailed for Plymouth, arriving on the 11th, when she was taken in hand for further repairs. Later in the month she joined the Home Fleet on the Clyde and on the 23rd sailed from the Clyde with the battleships *Nelson* and *Rodney* to carry out a search north of the Shetland Islands for the German battlecruisers *Scharnhorst* and *Gneisenau* after the sinking of the armed merchant cruiser *Rawalpindi*.

In December *Devonshire* transferred from Scapa Flow to Loch Ewe after the loss of the battleship *Royal Oak* to the German submarine *U47* but returned to Scapa Flow shortly before Christmas and in January 1940 was based on the Clyde. At the beginning of March, she became flagship of the 1st Cruiser Squadron Home Fleet, Vice-Admiral J H D Cunningham transferring

his flag. In April she deployed to Rosyth to embark troops of 1st/5th Royal Leicestershire Regiment for landings at Stavanger and Bergen (Operation R4), the operation being cancelled and the troops landed later, after the Germans had invaded Norway. After working with the French cruiser *Emile Bertin* off Kinnaird Head, she rejoined the main body of the fleet, and came under heavy air attacks off Bergen, sustaining only slight damage from a near miss but experiencing a very heavy expenditure of ammunition.

Devonshire moved to Narvik in support of operations pending the arrival of the main allied landing force (Operation Rupert), shortly afterwards forming part of the escort for French transports *Le D'Jezair*, *El Kantara* and *El Mansour* during the evacuation of Namsos, where she was subjected to air attacks and near missed. On June 6 *Devonshire* moved to Tromso to embark the Norwegian Royal Family, allied diplomats and members of the Norwegian government for passage to Great Britain, disembarking her passengers at Greenock.

In the middle of September *Devonshire* was deployed in an attempt to intercept the Vichy French cruisers *Montcalm*, *Georges Leygues* and *Gloire* but returned to Freetown after the Vichy French ships arrived in Dakar. With her sisters *Australia* and *Cumberland*, she ensured the enemy cruisers could not leave Dakar during the Free French landing operations, and took part, with other ships of Force M, in the bombardment of defences at Dakar. After the planned landings were cancelled, *Devonshire* returned to Freetown at the end of the month and, at the beginning of October she sailed from Freetown as part of the escort for the transport *Westralia* during her passage for landings by Free

French troops at Douala, French Cameroons. After providing cover for the landings, she returned to Freetown and transferred to the South Atlantic Station for further support of Free French operations, including the blockade of Gabon during the attack on Libreville. On 9 November, the Vichy French submarine *Poncelot* was attacked by the ship's aircraft.

During March to May 1941 *Devonshire* underwent a refit at Liverpool. She returned to her squadron at Scapa Flow in June and at the end of July participated in air attacks on shipping at Petsamo and Kirkenes, with the aircraft carriers *Furious* and *Victorious*, accompanied by her sister *Norfolk*. She remained with *Victorious* for her passage to Tromso and more air attacks, and then back to Scapa Flow, being present during the visit by HM King George VI on 9 August. On the 23rd of the month *Devonshire* deployed, with the aircraft carrier *Victorious* and her sister *Suffolk*, to provide cover for the passage of the first Russian convoy (PQ1) to Murmansk (Operation Dervish).

After refuelling at Spitzbergen, she joined the aircraft carrier *Victorious*, again with her sister *Suffolk*, for covering duties during air attacks at Hammerfest at the beginning of September. She then provided cover for the passage of the aircraft carrier *Argus* and her sister *Shropshire* to Archangel with aircraft and RAF personnel (Operation Strength). After once again refuelling at Spitzbergen, she rejoined *Victorious*, this time for air strikes on Bodo. In early November *Devonshire* was involved in the interception of a Vichy French convoy when five ships were captured and escorted to South Africa. Later in the month, as a result of the decryption of Enigma traffic, she intercepted the German commerce raider *Atlantis* north of Ascension Island. The German vessel was in the process of refuelling *U126* and *Devonshire* opened fire at long range obtaining hits. *Atlantis* scuttled herself and was abandoned, *Devonshire* subsequently withdrawing from the area at high speed because of threat of attack from *U126*.

In January 1942 *Devonshire* transferred to the US Navy Yard at Norfolk for repairs, returning to the Indian Ocean in March, where she joined US Navy vessels. In May she provided cover for the landings in Madagascar (Operation Ironclad), including the bombardment at Diego Suarez on the 7th, with the battleship *Ramillies* and the cruiser *Hermione*. After various convoy duties *Devonshire* returned to Great Britain for a refit in June 1943, and then rejoined the Home Fleet for work up at Scapa Flow, her next operation being to provide cover for the allied landings in Normandy (Operation Neptune) in June 1944.

In July she provided cover for unsuccessful air operations from the aircraft carriers *Formidable*, *Indefatigable* and *Furious* against the German battleship *Tirpitz*, then lying in Altenfjord, Norway (Operation Mascot). The following month,

with her sister *Kent*, *Devonshire* acted as escort for the aircraft carriers *Indefatigable*, *Nabob* and *Trumpeter* during Operation Offspring. Operation Goodwood, another air attack on *Tirpitz*, took place later in the month, *Devonshire* once again providing cover for the aircraft carriers, and at the beginning of September she joined her sisters *Kent* and *Berwick* as escort for the RMS *Queen Mary* which was taking the Prime Minister and Chiefs of Staff to USA for a meeting with the US President.

In May 1945 *Devonshire* escorted the minelayers *Apollo* and *Ariadne* from Rosyth to Oslo, *Apollo* carrying the Crown Prince of Norway on his return following VE Day. A month later *Devonshire* and her sister *Norfolk*, which was carrying HM King Haakon, repeated this same journey. From July 1945 to January 1946 *Devonshire* was deployed as a transport for the returning prisoners of war and allied nationals to Great Britain and service personnel to Australia. Later that year she was converted into a Cadet Training Ship at HM Dockyard, Devonport, and re-commissioned in April 1947, being used for training until October 1953, when she paid off; put on the disposal list in 1954, she was sold for breaking up later in the year.

HMS *LONDON*

Modifications. Between the wars *London* received the usual additions and in 1936/37 had undergone a substantial refit. However, for two years from March 1939 *London* underwent a major reconstruction by HM Dockyard, Chatham. The work included a new design of superstructure with aircraft hangars, cranes and a cross-deck catapult forward. The bridge was modernised and the funnel arrangements changed, only two remaining. Four twin 4in AA mountings, two 8-barrelled 2pdr pom-poms and two quad 0.5in AA guns were fitted. Air warning radar Type 279 was fitted on both masts and fire control radar for the forward main armament (Type 284) and for the 4in mountings (Type 285) provided with aerial units on the gunnery directors. Additional armour protection was added over the machinery spaces.

In a refit of October 1941 to January 1942 eight 20mm Oerlikon guns replaced the multiple machine guns. In another refit completed in May 1943 surface warning radar Type 273 was installed together with fire control radar Type 282, with aerials on the directors, for the 2pdr pom-pom mountings and seven additional 20mm Oerlikon mountings. The aircraft facilities were removed.

In January 1944, during a refit to suit her for British Pacific Fleet service, four twin 20mm mountings were fitted to improve close range AA defence and three singles removed. In mid-1945, radar Type 283 for barrage fire control was fitted and anti-aircraft armament modifications

included the installation of four single 40mm Bofors and four more twin 20mm, single Oerlikons being reduced to four. Radar Type 277 was fitted aft to replace the earlier Type 273 for surface warning.

Wartime highlights. *London* spent the beginning of the war undergoing a major rebuilding and it was not until 2 April 1941 that she deployed on the Northern Patrol for interception duties and began preparations for foreign service in the South Atlantic. The preparations were interrupted on a number of occasions, firstly to escort the aircraft carrier *Furious* to Gibraltar for Operation Splice, the delivery of aircraft to Malta, and to escort the SS *Arundel Castle*, which was taking evacuees from Gibraltar, back to Great Britain, and secondly to join the search for the German battleship *Bismarck* after the loss of the battlecruiser *Hood*. She did not begin operations in the South Atlantic until June when she was deployed in the search for German supply ships, intercepting the tanker *Esso Hamburg* on the 4th, the tanker being scuttled on *London*'s approach. Two other supply ships were also intercepted during June, the *Egerland* on the 6th and the *Babitonga* on the 21st.

In September *London* transferred to Iceland for duty with the Home Fleet and on the 22nd she embarked Lord Beaverbrook and Averill Harriman with an Anglo-American trade delegation for passage to Archangel, returning with the delegation whilst acting as part of the escort for the returning convoy QP1. In March 1942 *London* joined for Patrol White in the Denmark Strait with her sister *Kent* and three USN ships.

In the middle of May *London* sailed to Hvalfjord with the Home Fleet to meet the US battleship *Washington*, the cruiser *Tuscaloosa* and a screen of three USN destroyers, who had been detached for duty in support of the Home Fleet. On the 23rd she deployed with the battleships *Duke of York* and *Washington* and the aircraft carrier *Victorious* to provide cover for the passage of Russian convoy PQ16 and the returning convoy QP12.

At the beginning of July 1943, *London*, together with her sister *Kent* and the cruiser *Belfast*, was involved in an offensive sweep off Norway as a diversion during the Sicily landings (Operation Camera). After three months spent on interception duties, she sailed for the Mediterranean and in November collected members of the Defence Staff for their return to Great Britain after the Teheran Conference with US and Soviet leaders, arriving at the beginning of December. After a refit *London* sailed to

Ceylon to join the 4th Cruiser Squadron at Trincomalee in March 1944. Later in the month, she participated in an offensive sweep in the Indian Ocean (Operation Diplomat) and then met the US aircraft carrier *Saratoga* and three US destroyers which were joining the Eastern Fleet for temporary service. On 16 April *London* deployed with the battlecruiser *Renown* and the aircraft carriers *Illustrious* and *Saratoga* as TF70 for air attacks on Sabang. As part of TF67, *London* and her sister *Suffolk* escorted a tanker convoy to Exmouth Bay, Western Australia, to support TF65 during air operations against Soerabaya (Operation Transom).

From June *London* served as part of the 5th Cruiser Squadron on trade defence and interception duty in the Indian Ocean and on 15 October joined TG63.2, with her sisters *Suffolk* and *Cumberland*, for offensive operations in the Indian Ocean as a diversion during US landings on Leyte. In the middle of the month she bombarded targets in the Nicobars and came under attacks from torpedo carrying aircraft. In April 1945 *London* joined TF63 for offensive operations off Sumatra (Operation Sunfish). After a refit *London* took passage to Ceylon to rejoin the squadron in August. Landings in southern Malaya (Operation Zipper) were cancelled after the Japanese surrender and *London* was diverted to Rangoon to await further instructions. On 28 August she anchored 5 miles from Sabang with the battleship *Nelson* and received charts of the Japanese minefields off Malaya and Singapore from the Japanese delegation. On the 31st the surrender of the Japanese forces in Sumatra was carried out on board and on 2 September she landed Royal Marines for the occupation of Sabang and then sailed to Singapore.

London remained on station until January 1946 when she returned to Great Britain and was deployed for trooping duties to bring personnel back to Great Britain from Sydney and Singapore. In September 1946 she paid off and was reduced to reserve status at Chatham. She then refitted for further service with the British Pacific Fleet and, after working-up in the Mediterranean, joined the 5th

Cruiser Squadron at Hong Kong in 1947. During the next two years *London* was deployed on fleet duties including the protection of British flagged ships trading in Chinese waters. The most notable event in this period was the attempt to rescue the sloop *Amethyst*, which had been trapped in the Yangtse River. Whilst in action against Chinese Communist shore batteries with the sloop *Black Swan*, *London* was hit by 23 shells which caused major damage. *London* returned to Shanghai and then to Great Britain in June 1949, arriving in Chatham in September where she was placed on the disposal list and sold in January 1950.

HMS *SHROPSHIRE*

Modifications. Modernised along the lines of *Devonshire* in 1936-37, her AA armament was enhanced by the installation of four further 4in single mountings and two quad 0.5in MGs, with an additional HACS on the forward director platform. She received two 8-barrelled pom-poms in spring 1941. In early 1942 radar Type 281 for air warning, Type 273 for surface warning, Type 285 for fire control of the secondary armament and Type 282 for control of the close range AA armament were fitted, and the single 4in mountings were replaced by twin mountings; the close range AA defence was supplemented by single 20mm Oerlikon guns (she had ten by the end of the year). The aircraft facilities were removed in a 1942/43 refit, when the AA fit became seven twin and six single 20mm Oerlikons.

In June 1944 her torpedo tubes were removed and an additional 20mm Oerlikon gun fitted. Between April and May 1945, all the 20mm AA guns were replaced by thirteen single 40mm weapons, a surface warning radar Type 293 replaced the previous Type 273 and the Type 277 fire control radar for the main armament was replaced.

Wartime highlights. *Shropshire* was stationed in the Mediterranean on the outbreak of war and carried out contraband control patrols there to enforce the blockade of enemy shipping and cargoes destined for German ports, but in October transferred to

An aerial view of *London* at sea in August 1942, with her Walrus being prepared for flight. By this date the 0.5in MGs have been removed and single 20mm Oerlikons positioned on B and X turrets; the other 20mm positions are, sided, in the bridge wings and two on the after superstructure, making eight in all. The Type 273 lantern can be seen just ahead of the mainmast.

the South Atlantic command for interception of commerce raiders and trade defence. After arriving at Simonstown in the middle of the month, *Shropshire*, with her sister *Sussex*, formed part of a hunting group searching for the German battleship *Admiral Graf Spee*, which was operating off South Africa. In early December she again operated with her sister *Sussex* in the Indian Ocean and on 9 December intercepted the German blockade runner *Adolf Leonhardt*, which scuttled herself to avoid capture. In January 1940 *Shropshire*, with her sister *Dorsetshire*, acted as escort for the damaged cruiser *Exeter* during her passage in the South Atlantic on her return to Great Britain.

In the middle of July *Shropshire* took part in a search for German warships in the North Sea, with her sister *Sussex* and the cruisers *Southampton* and *Glasgow*, the search being cancelled when a report that the German warships had reversed course was received but, during their return to Scapa Flow, *Glasgow* was involved in a collision with the destroyer *Imogen*, which was sunk. On 21 January 1941 *Shropshire* joined military convoy WS5A at Capetown as escort during its passage to Durban and on to Aden. Owing to the outbreak of disease on board, she was withdrawn from patrol duties and sailed to Durban for control of the epidemic. Even though some of the ship's complement were only considered fit for light duties because of the epidemic, she rejoined Force T in early February and provided support for military operations in Somaliland, including the bombardment of Italian positions at Mogadishu on the 14th.

On the 22nd *Shropshire* joined her sisters *Australia* and *Canberra* and the cruisers *Glasgow*, *Emerald* and *Enterprise* to carry out a search for the German battleship *Admiral Scheer* and on 2 March inter-cepted the Vichy French freighter *Ville De Strasbourg*, which was taken as a prize. She returned to Simonstown, after replenishing at Durban, and was under refit during April. The post-refit trials revealed a number of defects and she returned to Simonstown for further repairs, moving to Freetown in early June, where she embarked German prisoners of war for passage to Great Britain. The prisoners were disembarked on 5 July after arrival at Scapa Flow and *Shropshire* sailed to Hvalfjord at the end of the month.

On 18 August *Shropshire* took passage from Hvalfjord to Scapa Flow with the battleships *Prince of Wales*, which was taking the Prime Minister Winston Churchill back to Great Britain from the Atlantic Charter meeting with the US President Franklin Roosevelt, and *Ramillies*, the depot ship *Hecla* and five destroyers. Although intended to receive a refit in September, *Shropshire* escorted the aircraft carrier *Argus*, which was taking Hurricane aircraft and RAF personnel for duties in North Russia (Operation Strength), to Archangel. She joined her sister *London* as part of the escort for convoy QP1 during its passage from Archangel and then received a refit.

The first part of 1942 was spent under-going repairs and in September *Shropshire* was offered to the Royal Australian Navy as a replacement for the cruiser *Canberra*, which had been sunk after damage in an action against Japanese warships at Savo Island on 9 August. Following a refit, she re-commissioned as HMAS *Shropshire* on 20 April 1943 and in October was nomi-nated for service with TF74 under US Navy command. At the end of the month, she joined her sister *Australia* and the cruiser *Hobart* at Brisbane as part of TF74 and in November supported the assault on

Bougainville at Point Purvis. In the middle of December she provided cover for landings by the 112th US Cavalry at Arawe, New Britain (Operation Director). At the end of the month she covered landing of the 1st US Marine Division and bombarded assault beaches, receiving praise from the command for her accuracy (Operation Dexterity).

In January 1944 she covered landing by the 32nd US Infantry Division near Saidor, New Guinea and at the end of the month received a well deserved leave period in Sydney. At the beginning of February *Shropshire* relieved her sister *Australia* as flagship of TF74 and on 3 March sailed to the Admiralty Islands where she bombarded gun positions on Hauwei and Nbrilo Islands at the entrance to Seeadler Harbour during the assault on the Admiralty Islands by the 5th US Cavalry. In the middle of April, she took passage from Milne Bay to Sudest with TF74 for joint operations under TF77 command for support of the landings in Dutch New Guinea and later in the month provided naval gunfire support at Tanamera Bay. Further bombardment of enemy positions took place in the middle of May and she again provided naval gunfire support on the 27th, this time in support of the landings by the 41st US Infantry Division on the south coast of Biak.

Because of a defective propeller shaft *Shropshire* was withdrawn from operations and took passage to Sydney for repair and refit, on completion of which she rejoined TF74, arriving at Humboldt Bay in early July. In the middle of July *Shropshire*, together with her sister *Australia*, bombarded Japanese positions opposing the US advance. At the beginning of September she joined TG75.2 with *Australia* and two Australian destroyers and in the middle of the month was deployed in support of landings by 31st and 32nd US Divisions of the XI Corps at Morotai in the Moluccas, based at Biak, providing naval gunfire support.

In October she was allocated to TG77.2 and sailed from Manus for Hollandia to support ships of TF78 during the US assault on Leyte. On the 21st of the month, she replaced her damaged sister *Australia* as senior RAN ship and on the 24th was part of a force in action with Japanese warships *Mogami*, *Shigure* and *Yamashiro* during the Battle of Leyte Gulf, all the enemy ships being sunk. At the end of the month *Shropshire* joined TG77.1 in support of landings by providing naval gunfire support and carrying out patrols to intercept any Japanese attempt to prevent landings. On 1 November she came under Kamikaze attacks and was near missed by an aircraft which then sank a nearby US Navy destroyer. At the beginning of December *Shropshire* joined TG74.1 with her sister *Australia* and covered landings on Mindoro by the 503rd Parachute Regiment. After a period for 'rest and recuperation' at Palua Island she joined TG77.2 for support of landings at Lingayen Gulf at the beginning of 1945 and again came under Kamikaze attacks, suffering two near misses.

Landing support continued until 1 March when the RAN squadron disbanded and *Shropshire* received a refit at Sydney which lasted until June. On the 13th she joined TG74.1 at Tawi Tawi and on the 18/19th bombarded Labuan Island, followed by general support off Borneo. From the 27th until 1 July she bombarded various shore targets and then returned to Tawi Tawi to replenish. Further bombardments followed until another period for 'rest and recuperation' later in July, this time at Manila. On 26 July *Shropshire* rejoined TF74 at Subic Bay and remained there until after the Japanese surrender on 17 August, when she took passage to Japan via Manila and Okinawa.

Shropshire was deployed in the transfer of repatriated British and Commonwealth POWs from Japan until November 1945 when she was relieved by HMAS *Hobart*. She carried the Australian contingent to Great Britain for the victory celebrations, arriving at Portsmouth on 30 May 1946 and returning with them during August. After a refit in Sydney the ship made one more trip to Japan before paying off into reserve at Sydney in April 1947. During 1954 *Shropshire* was sold.

HMS *SUSSEX*

Modifications. Before the war this ship received much the same modifications as *Shropshire*. Badly damaged in October 1940, a long period of repair was only

Shropshire in Sydney harbour at the end of the war. The ship has had her torpedo tubes removed and the AA armament considerably strengthened by the fitting of single 40mm Bofors (as many as fifteen in some records, but at least twelve can be made out in this photo). All the 20mm were removed.

completed in July 1942, when radar equipment for surface and aircraft warning and for fire control of both secondary and AA armament was fitted. The single 4in were replaced by four twins, and ten 20mm Oerlikon guns and two 8-barrelled pom-pom mountings were installed to improve close range defence against air attacks. In November she received a fire control radar for the main armament and replacement of the surface warning radar by an improved design, which was sited on the after superstructure to improve cover.

The ship then received no significant alteration until a major refit between January and February 1945 when extensive changes were made, including the removal of X turret aft, the aircraft facilities and torpedo tubes. More modern radars were also installed, including barrage fire control, and the siting of the close range AA weapons was improved. These latter now comprised six octuple 2pdr pom-poms, four twin and four single 20mm Oerlikons.

Wartime highlights. At the start of war *Sussex* transferred to the East Indies station for trade protection duties. In early November she joined her sister *Shropshire* in a search for the German battleship *Admiral Graf Spee* in the South Atlantic and then transferred to the River Plate area before moving to the Indian Ocean to continue the search. On 2 December, whilst with the battlecruiser *Renown*, she intercepted the German merchant ship *Watussi* (which scuttled herself) and the search continued with her sister *Shropshire* between St Helena and the Cape of Good Hope. At the end of the month she transferred to the 4th Cruiser Squadron and took passage to Colombo, arriving there on 6 January 1940, transferring to Home Waters for service with the 1st Cruiser Squadron, Home Fleet in March. After a refit and on completion of sea trials in May, she joined the squadron at Scapa Flow and was deployed to intercept any German ships attempting to break out into the Atlantic via the NW Approaches. In June she escorted evacuation convoys from Norway and in mid-July took part in a search for enemy ships in the North Sea with her sister *Shropshire* and the cruiser *Southampton*, the operation being called off when the enemy ships reversed course. In August a machinery defect was discovered and *Sussex* went to Glasgow for repairs to her turbine blades. Whilst there she was hit in the engine room by a 250-pound bomb that caused a serious fire, threatening the magazines. Because of the danger of an explosion, the local community was evacuated and the dry dock was flooded. The subsequent flooding of compartments made the ship unstable and she capsized.

The extensive structural damage was repaired at Govan, repairs taking until the end of July 1942 when *Sussex* rejoined the 1st Cruiser Squadron at Scapa Flow but in November she was withdrawn from service for further refit work in a Tyne shipyard, rejoining the 1st Cruiser Squadron at Scapa Flow in January 1943 and then transferring to the 4th Cruiser Squadron, Eastern Fleet. During her passage to Mombasa she intercepted the German tanker *Hohen Friedburg* SW of Cape Finisterre and came under torpedo attack by *U264* but was able to avoid a salvo of four torpedoes. The year 1943 was spent undertaking convoy escort duties and undergoing refit at Durban.

In April 1944 *Sussex* transferred to Home waters for a refit, which lasted until March 1945 when she carried out post-refit trials and was nominated for service with the 5th Cruiser Squadron, Eastern Fleet. After work up with the Mediterranean Fleet she took passage to join the Eastern Fleet at Trincomalee in July. On the 19th she joined the battleship *Nelson* and the aircraft carriers *Empress* and *Ameer* to form TF63 and cover minesweeping operations by the 4th Minesweeping Flotilla off Phuket Island and a series of air strikes by the aircraft carriers on the Kra Isthmus (Operation Livery).

On the 26th *Sussex* came under

Sussex at anchor in the mid-1930s, after the fitting of the catapult (1931/32) but before the refit of 1936/37. *(National Maritime Museum N20828)*

Kamikaze attack, during which two aircraft were destroyed and *Sussex* sustained slight structural damage above the waterline from the wreckage of a Japanese aircraft. In August she prepared for Malayan landings (Operation Zipper) and at the end of the month sailed to Singapore for its re-occupation, acting as flagship for the Occupation Force (Operation Tiderace). On 4 September she arrived off Singapore with the Landing Ship (Infantry) *Kedah* and ships of the 7th Minesweeping Flotilla, the subsequent surrender of Japanese forces by Lt-Gen Itagaki and Vice Admiral Fukudone being accepted on board.

On 12 September *Sussex* was present at the formal surrender of Japan to the Supreme Commander, SEAC by General Itakagi, and she remained at Singapore during the landing of the 3rd Commando Brigade. *Sussex* remained with the Eastern Fleet after VJ Day and provided cover for the landings of the 5th Indian Division at Soerabaya, Java in November 1945. Before her return to Great Britain, she supported military operations against insurgents in Java. Having been nominated for use as a troopship she returned to Chatham late in March 1946 and, after essential changes to suit this role, she carried personnel returning from the Far East until she was paid-off at Devonport prior to refit. On completion of the refit in April 1947 she re-commissioned for service in the 5th Cruiser Squadron, British Pacific Fleet, working up at Malta. At the end of 1948 she was relieved by the cruiser *Belfast* and returned to go into reserve at Portsmouth, where she was de-equipped and placed on the disposal list, being sold in January 1950.

HMS *DORSETSHIRE*

Modifications. As with the *London* class, the planned pre-war refits for *Dorsetshire* and *Norfolk* were abandoned but they did receive aircraft facilities and their single 4in AA guns were replaced by twin mountings. In June 1941 air warning radar was fitted to *Dorsetshire*, and she had nine single 20mm by the time of her loss.

Wartime highlights. *Dorsetshire* was serving with the 5th Cruiser Squadron on the China Station when war broke out in 1939. In October she transferred to the East Indies Station, arriving at Colombo on the 25th of the month where she joined her sister *Cornwall* and the cruiser *Gloucester*. After a number of unsuccessful searches for the German battleship *Admiral Graf Spee*, she transferred to the South Atlantic Station at the beginning of December. On 19 December *Dorsetshire* was ordered to join the cruisers *Achilles* (RNZN), *Ajax* and *Exeter* off Montevideo after their action with *Graf Spee*, joining them at Port Stanley in the Falklands on the 24th. She sailed from there with her sister *Cumberland* on the 29th and joined another sister, *Shropshire*, in early January 1940, remaining off Montevideo. Following gunnery exercises with *Ajax* and *Shropshire*, she escorted the damaged cruiser *Exeter* to Great Britain and then returned to the South Atlantic for further patrol duties with her sister *Shropshire*. On 12 February, her aircraft intercepted the German freighter *Wakama* off Cape Frio.

In March *Dorsetshire* took the wounded from the cruiser *Exeter* to Capetown. Following refits she joined the aircraft carrier *Hermes* for surveillance of the French warships at Dakar on 23 June, shadowing the French battleship *Richelieu* during her passage from Dakar to Casablanca two days later. On 8 July she deployed with her sister *Australia* to provide cover during the attack on *Richelieu* at Dakar. On 24 July *Dorsetshire* intercepted a Portuguese ship and detained the Italian Consul who was a passenger, landing him at Freetown five days later.

In the middle of November she supported the military operations in Somaliland, including the bombardment of Dante. In December she joined the cruiser *Neptune* to search for the German battleship *Admiral Scheer*, after the SS *Duquesa* had made a raider report. On 21 January 1941 *Dorsetshire* intercepted the Vichy French SS *Mendoza* and put a prize crew on board, sending the ship to Freetown. The

Sussex on 4 April 1945 after the refit that removed X turret, the torpedo tubes and aircraft. The light AA is now disposed as follows: the 8-barrelled 2pdr pom-poms, in shielded mountings, are sited abreast the forward funnel, mainmast and, sided, where X turret had been; from forward, the 20mm Oerlikons are on B turret (two singles), two on platforms ahead of the bridge, a twin each side of the bridge on the shelter deck level, two twins between the second and third funnels, and a single on a platform between the after two pom-pom mountings, port and starboard.

The foremast carries Type 277 surface search and, at the masthead, Type 293 target indication radars, and there is an extensive suite of fire control radars.

Midships detail of *Dorsetshire* in 1933. The aircraft is a Fairey IIIF three-seater spotter-reconnaissance floatplane (serial number S1833) on an EIIH catapult. The recently added quad Vickers 0.5in machine guns can be seen between the first two funnels, and it is just possible to make out one of the single 2pdr pom-poms abreast the after end of the bridge at shelter-deck level. *(National Maritime Museum N8338)*

prize crew did not rejoin the ship until the beginning of February and in March, whilst at the Seychelles, the ship's Walrus aircraft crashed on shore, killing four naval personnel and one civilian. On 6 May *Dorsetshire* rescued 35 survivors from the SS *Oakdene*, which had been torpedoed by a submarine earlier that day. Towards the end of the month she joined the search for the German battleship *Bismarck* after the sinking of the battlecruiser *Hood*. On the 27th she engaged *Bismarck*, along with the battleships *Rodney* and *King George V*, finally sinking her with torpedoes after she had been demolished by surface gunfire.

Following a refit, she was present on 9 August for the royal visit by HM King George VI to the Home Fleet at Scapa Flow. On 21 September the ship's Walrus aircraft crashed whilst she was in company with the aircraft carrier *Eagle*, and she embarked a new aircraft at Freetown. On 1 December *Dorsetshire* sighted the German U-boat supply ship *Python* with submarines *UA* and *U68* alongside. The submarines departed and made torpedo attacks, which failed, and *Python* was scuttled. In March 1942 *Dorsetshire* deployed in support of military operations to evacuate personnel from Burma, including the landing of a Royal Marines detachment to man motor launches of the Inshore Flotilla during evacuation of allied troops to Akyab from Burma.

At the end of the month she sailed to Colombo for a refit and entered dry dock but on the 31st the work was suspended when Japanese surface ships were reported in the Indian Ocean. *Dorsetshire* undocked

and sailed from Colombo but on 2 April returned to Ceylon to continue the refit. On the 4th she was recalled by the C-in-C Eastern Fleet to join Force A and the next day was sighted by aircraft from the Japanese cruiser *Tone*. She then came under heavy dive-bombing attacks from carrier aircraft and sank within 8 minutes, 234 of the ship's company losing their lives.

HMS *NORFOLK*

Modifications. Pre-war the ship was refitted to the same standard as *Dorsetshire*. She had UP mountings added to B and X turret in June 1940, and in October was fitted with radar Type 286M. The UP mountings and 0.5in MGs were removed during the refit of July–September 1941 and four 20mm singles added. In October 1942 Type 273 radar was fitted (positioned before the bridge) and three more 20mm added. A more substantial refit in March to May 1943 removed the catapult (allowing the Type 273 to be moved aft) and increased the 20mm Oerlikons to eighteen singles. In November 1944 the ship emerged from a major refit having lost X turret and the 8-barrelled pom-poms, which had been replaced by six quadruple pom-poms, eleven twin 20mm and ten singles. A final refit in 1945 gave the ship ten single 40mm Bofors in lieu of the single 20mm.

Wartime highlights. On 6 September 1939 *Norfolk* joined the 8th Cruiser Squadron of the Home Fleet and at the end of the month she formed part of the covering force to

Norfolk in June 1943 sporting a three-colour camouflage scheme of B30, G45 and B55. Just out of refit at Portsmouth, the ship has had the catapult removed and the prominent lantern of the Type 273 radar moved aft from its original position behind B turret (an unpopular arrangement as it restricted the view from the bridge). A large number of single 20mm Oerlikons was also added and fire control radar enhanced.

escort the submarine *Spearfish*, which had been damaged during patrol in the North Sea. In October she transferred to the 1st Cruiser Squadron in the Mediterranean, along with her sisters *Devonshire*, *Suffolk* and *Berwick*. Having sailed to Alexandria with *Suffolk*, she was ordered to return to the Home Fleet at the beginning of November, and on the 23rd she joined in a search for the German battleships *Scharnhorst* and *Gneisenau* after the sinking of the armed merchant cruiser *Rawalpindi*. On the 27th *Norfolk* was attacked by *U47* off the Orkney Islands but the torpedoes exploded astern.

On 16 March 1940 *Norfolk* intercepted the German ship *Uruguay*, which scuttled herself, but after return to Scapa Flow she came under air attack and was hit on the port side of the quarterdeck abreast Y turret, the bomb exploding in the shell room. She underwent repairs in the Clyde and rejoined the 1st Cruiser Squadron at the end of June. In November after a short period of repair, she returned to Scapa Flow and in December took part in an unsuccessful search off Freetown for the German cruiser *Admiral Hipper*.

During January 1941 *Norfolk* carried out a search for the German raider *Kormoran* in the South Atlantic. In the middle of May she joined her sister *Suffolk* in a search for the

Norfolk entering Malta in October 1945. The ship underwent two substantial changes to AA and electronics fit in 1944 and 1945, the main features being six quad 2pdrs replacing the two octuple mounts, and later ten 40mm Bofors in place of the same number of single 20mm. Note the simplified camouflage scheme adopted by many warships later in the war. *(Wright & Logan Collection)*

German battleship *Bismarck*. She made the first sighting report of *Bismarck*, came under fire, but continued to shadow *Bismarck* and *Prinz Eugen* until the enemy ships were lost in a snow storm. *Norfolk* was detached to refuel but was recalled after *Bismarck* was located again and she later engaged *Bismarck* along with the battleships *King George V* and *Rodney*.

In the middle of May 1942 *Norfolk* formed part of the escort for the battleship *Duke of York* and the aircraft carrier *Victorious* which were covering the return of the damaged cruiser *Trinidad* from Murmansk and came under air attack on the return passage. In October she was detached to cover military convoys to Gibraltar for the allied landings in North Africa (Operation Torch) and in July 1943 *Norfolk* took part in a diversionary offensive sweep off the Norwegian coast with the battleship *Anson* and the US battleship *Alabama*, as a diversion during the allied landings in Sicily (Operations Convent and Camera). In mid-August she provided cover for mining by ships of the 1st Minelaying Squadron in the Northern Barrage (Operation SN74) and also for a special operation related to Russian convoy defence (Operation Lorry). In mid-September she was involved in the relief of the Spitzbergen garrison (Operation EH), together with the battleship *Anson* and the US aircraft carrier *Ranger*. On Boxing Day *Norfolk* took part in the sinking of the German battleship *Scharnhorst*, being hit twice by enemy fire which damaged both X turret and her radar equipment, seven of the ship's company being killed and five wounded.

The majority of 1944 was spent undergoing a refit on the Tyne and in mid-January 1945 *Norfolk* joined Force 1 for an offensive sweep off the coast of Norway (Operation Spellbinder) and in mid-February covered the aerial mining off Skatestrommen by aircraft from the aircraft carriers *Premier* and *Puncher* and air attacks on shipping off Bud (Operation Selenium). At the beginning of May *Norfolk* provided cover for an air strike on shipping targets west of Narvik by aircraft from the escort carriers *Queen*, *Searcher* and *Trumpeter* (Operation Judgement). On the 6th she covered the transit through the Skagerrak of the cruisers *Birmingham* and *Dido* which were on passage to Copenhagen for the re-occupation.

On 15 May she embarked Vice Admiral R R McGrigor for passage to Bergen and on 5 June carried King Haakon of Norway for passage to Oslo (Operation Indestructible). Having undergone a refit, *Norfolk* went to work up in Malta during October 1945 prior to joining the 5th Cruiser Squadron in the East Indies. She joined the squadron as flagship in December 1945 and remained on station until 1949 when, she paid-off into reserve before being laid up at Falmouth and sold in January 1950 for demolition.

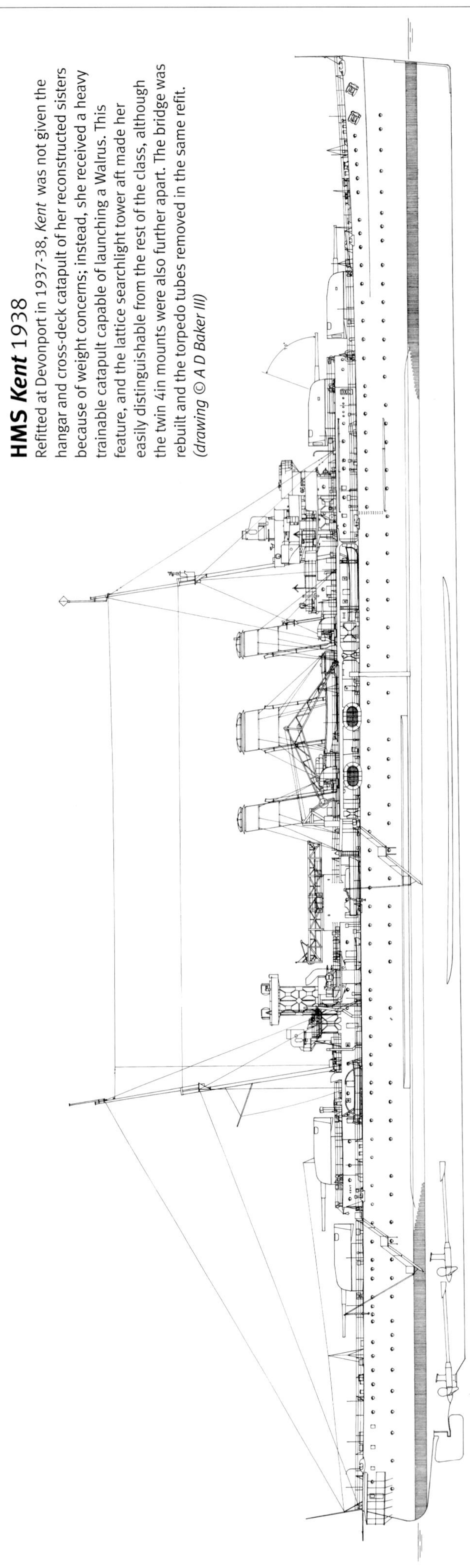

HMS *Kent* 1938

Refitted at Devonport in 1937-38, *Kent* was not given the hangar and cross-deck catapult of her reconstructed sisters because of weight concerns; instead, she received a heavy trainable catapult capable of launching a Walrus. This feature, and the lattice searchlight tower aft made her easily distinguishable from the rest of the class, although the twin 4in mounts were also further apart. The bridge was rebuilt and the torpedo tubes removed in the same refit.
(*drawing* © *A D Baker III*)

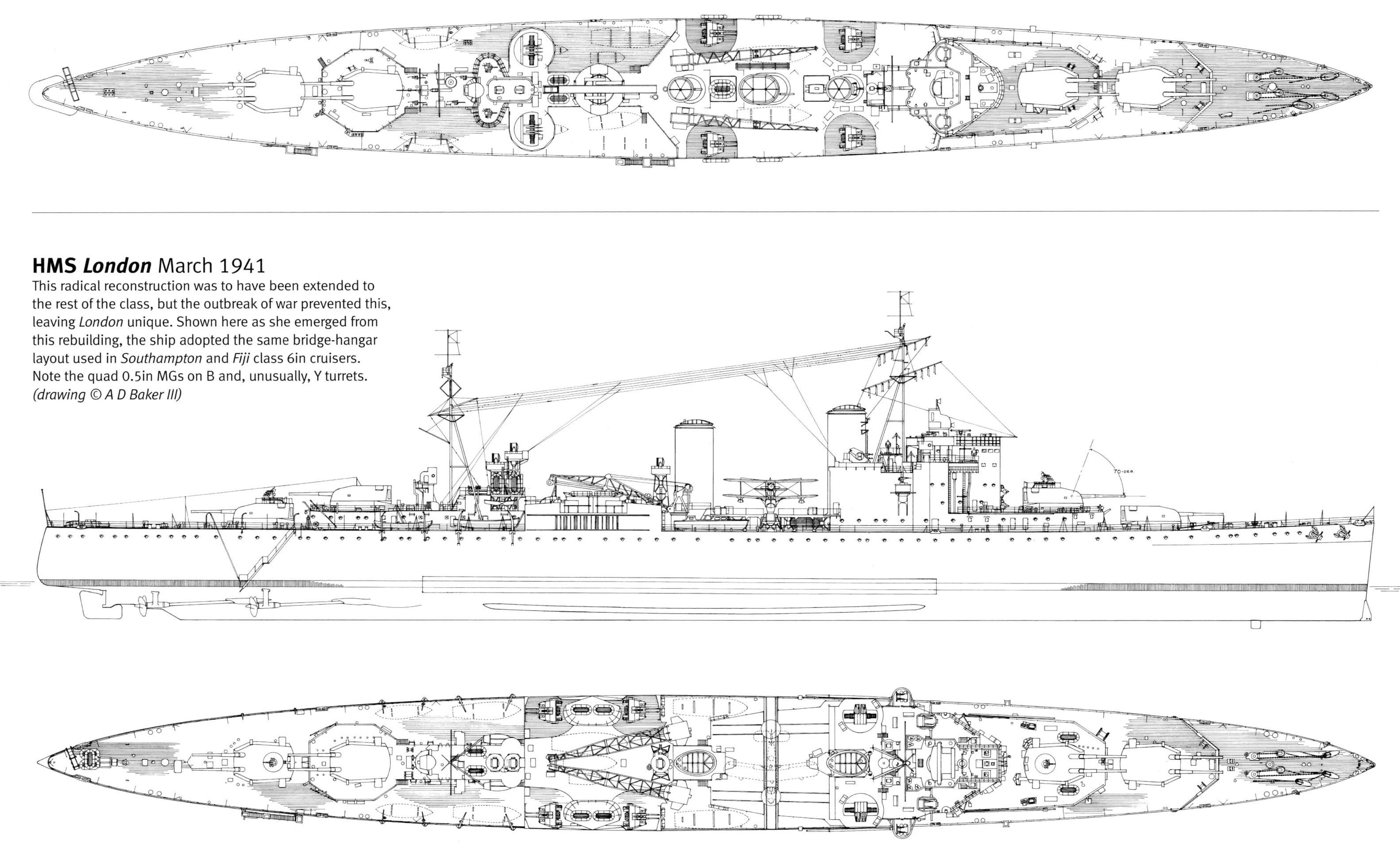

HMS *London* March 1941

This radical reconstruction was to have been extended to the rest of the class, but the outbreak of war prevented this, leaving *London* unique. Shown here as she emerged from this rebuilding, the ship adopted the same bridge-hangar layout used in *Southampton* and *Fiji* class 6in cruisers. Note the quad 0.5in MGs on B and, unusually, Y turrets. *(drawing © A D Baker III)*

Selected References

Below are listed just some of the many publications with significant information on 'County' class cruisers. All of them include photographs of the ships and these are worth close study if an accurate model of a particular vessel at a specific time in her career is to be produced. Many of them also include drawings of the vessels, unfortunately often only at small scales but again these are worth close study. The Profile Morskie series of books do include larger scale detailed drawings and camouflage patterns but concern has been expressed at the absolute accuracy of the information contained in them and, as always, it is worth checking with dated photographs to confirm details.

HMS London by Iain Ballantyne (Barnsley 2002, ISBN 0 85052 843 7)

HMS Cumberland by Patrick Boniface (Penzance 2006, ISBN 1 904381 37 5)

Cruisers of World War Two by M J Whitley (London 1995, ISBN 1 85409 225 1)

Profile Morskie 77: HMS Kent by Slawomir Brzezinski (Wyszków 2006, ISBN 83 87918 74 1)

Profile Morskie 91: HMS London by Slawomir Brzezinski (Wyszków 2007, ISBN 978 83 60590 91 1)

Nelson to Vanguard: Warship Design and Development 1923-1945, by D K Brown (London 2000, ISBN 1 86176 136 8)

Conway's All The World's Fighting Ships, 1922-1946, edited by Roger Chesneau (London & New York 1980, ISBN 0 85177 146 7)

British Cruisers: Two World Wars and After by Norman Friedman (Barnsley & Annapolis 2010, ISBN 978 1 84832 078 9)

Okrety Swiata 7: Brytyjskie Krazowniki Cekkie Typu 'County' by Jacek Jarosz (Poland 1999, ISBN 83 908942 1 1)

Treaty Cruisers by Leo Marriot (Barnsley 2005, ISBN 1 84415 188 3)

Cruisers of the Royal and Commonwealth Navies since 1879 by Douglas Morris (Liskeard 1987, ISBN 0 907771 35 1)

Man O'War 1: County Class Cruisers by Alan Raven and John Roberts (New York 1978, ISBN 0 85368 213 5)

British Cruisers of World War Two by Alan Raven and John Roberts (London 1980, ISBN 0 85368 304 2)

Yesterday's Navy by Lt Cdr Ben Warlow RN (Liskeard 2009, ISBN 978 1 904459 37 8)

MODEL MANUFACTURERS

NAVIS MODELLBAU
Dr I Kraus
Mozartweg 2
D-82538 Geretsried
Germany
www.navis-neptun.de

HP MODELS
Postfach 101151
46471 Wesel
Germany
www.hp-models.com

WHITE ENSIGN MODELS LTD
South Farm, Snitton, Ludlow
Shropshire, SY8 3EZ
England
www.whiteensignmodels.com

SKYTREX LIMITED
Unit 1, Charnwood Business Park
North Road
Loughborough, LE11 1LE
United Kingdom
www.skytrex.com

L'ARSENAL
Boîte Postal No2
14790 Verson
France
www.larsenal.com

COMMANDER SERIES MODELS, INC.
551 Wegman Road, Rochester
NY 14624MODELKOK
USA
www.commanderseries.com

METCALF MOULDINGS
1 Wentworth Cottages,
Haultwick, Dane End,
Nr. Ware, Herts., SG11 1JG.
England
http://business.virgin.net/metcalf.mouldings/catalogue.htm

FLEETSCALE
Westward Mouldings Ltd
The New Factory, Greenhill
Delaware Road, Gunnislake
Cornwall, PL18 9AS
United Kingdom
www.fleetscale.com

GOLD MEDAL MODELS
P.O. Box 670, Lopez, WA 98261
USA
http://goldmm.com/

TOM'S MODELWORKS
P.O. Box 304, Santa Rosa
CA 95402
USA
www.tomsmodelworks.com

EDUARD MODEL-ACCESSORIES
Mírová 170, 43521 Obrnice
Czech Republic
www.eduard.cz

AIRFIX
Customer Care
Hornby Hobbies Ltd, Westwood
Margate, Kent, CT9 4JX
United Kingdom
www.airfix.com

QUAYCRAFT
73 Chambercombe Road
Ilfracombe
North Devon, EX34 9PH
United Kingdom
www.quaycraft.co.uk

MARCLE MODELS
Turnagain, Finch Lane, Amersham
Buckinghamshire, HP7 9NE
United Kingdom
www.marcle.co.uk

GHQ
28100 Woodside Road
Shorewood
MN 55331
USA
www.ghqmodels.com

Clydeside Flotilla
3A Ferry Road, Millport
Isle of Cumbrae,
Scotland
KA28 OD7
United Kingdom
www.clydeside-flotilla.com

COMBRIG
www.combrig-models.com

MOUNTFORD METAL MINIATURES LTD.
14 Cherry Tree Drive
Duckmanton
Chesterfield, S44 5JL
United Kingdom
www.mountfordminiatures.com